D0274057

BS

LEABHARLANNA CHONTAE NA GAILLIMHE
(GALWAY COUNTY LIBRARIES)

Acc. No......D185589...... Class No....338·0941 5

Date of Return	Date of Return	Date of Return

THAT'LL NEVER WORK ...
SUCCESS STORIES FROM PRIVATE IRISH BUSINESS

GALWAY COUNTY LIBRARIES

THAT'LL NEVER WORK ...
SUCCESS STORIES FROM PRIVATE IRISH BUSINESS

Michael Gaffney and Colin O'Brien

MERCIER PRESS
WHAT YOU NEED TO READ

MERCIER PRESS
Cork
www.mercierpress.ie

Trade enquiries to CMD Distribution,
55A Spruce Avenue, Stillorgan Industrial Park, Blackrock, County
Dublin.

© Michael Gaffney & Colin O'Brien, 2008
Photographs © Mark McCall, 2008 except for photo of Richard Barrett
© Treasury Holdings

ISBN: 978 1 85635 569 8

10 9 8 7 6 5 4 3 2

GALWAY COUNTY LIBRARIES

A CIP record for this title is available from the British Library

arts
council
schomhairle Mercier Press receives financial assistance from the Arts Council/
ealaíon An Chomhairle Ealaíon

185.589   €15.00

This book is sold subject to the condition that it shall not, by way of trade or otherwise, be lent, resold, hired out or otherwise circulated without the publisher's prior
consent in any form of binding or cover other than that in which it is published
and without a similar condition including this condition being imposed on the
subsequent purchaser.

No part of this publication may be reproduced or transmitted in any form or by any
means, electronic or mechanical, including photocopying, recording or any information or retrieval system, without the prior permission of the publisher in writing.

The information contained herein is of a general nature. It is not intended to
address the circumstances of any particular individual or entity and does not
constitute professional advice. While every care has been taken in the prepara-
tion of the information in this book, there can be no guarantee that such information is accurate. No one should act upon such information without appropriate
professional advice after a thorough examination of the particular situation and
readers are advised to seek specific professional advice in relation to any decision
or course of action. Unless otherwise stated, opinions are those of the contributors and are not necessarily endorsed by KPMG or the authors.

©2008 KPMG, an Irish partnership and a member firm of the KPMG network
of independent member firms affiliated with KPMG International, a Swiss cooperative. All rights reserved. KPMG and the KPMG logo are registered trade-
marks of KPMG International, a Swiss cooperative.

Printed and bound by J.H. Haynes & Co. Ltd, Sparkford

Contents

Acknowledgements

The most important people to thank are all our contributors for giving us their time and their story. It has been a great experience and one we thoroughly enjoyed. Thank you also to our many KPMG colleagues, especially Elaine Hickey-Dwyer, who ably assisted in the editing task and kept the production on schedule. And finally our thanks to Mark McCall for his wonderful photography.

Foreword

Sean FitzPatrick,
Chairman, Anglo Irish Bank

This book is a collection of stories. They are very personal stories, told by people in their own words, with an honesty and sense of humour and with one common theme.

That theme is success. Success derived from some combination of hard work, luck, risk taking, enterprise and innovation, all mixed up into a solution that worked for the individual. In some cases there was a grand plan, in many other cases success was achieved as much by accident as design.

These stories help answer a question I am regularly asked – what is an entrepreneur and how can I be one?

If you are looking for a definition of an entrepreneur, these stories may help you answer that question. Above all, they highlight that there is no one simple definition and, given that everyone's circumstances are different, everyone's opportunities will be unique to them.

These stories show that having the right attitude, ambition and the resolve to achieve your goals will bring out the entrepreneur in you, no matter what your role is. Whether you are in business or in the public service, whether you are young or old, experienced or inexperienced – you can think and act like an entrepreneur.

I congratulate the contributors on their success and hope that their stories inspire others to take the plunge and pursue their dreams and enjoy the game of life.

Preface
Michael Gaffney & Colin O'Brien

The lifeblood of the economy is the private sector and particularly those – mostly unsung – heroes who build up and run businesses.

Irish entrepreneurs have played a pivotal role in the development of Ireland into an economic powerhouse over the last few decades. They have shown remarkable confidence and taken enormous personal risks. They have taken on a role in Irish life unprecedented in previous times.

In KPMG, we every day come upon fascinating people who have started a business from scratch, taken over a small enterprise and built it to formidable scale, or re-invigorated a stalled home-grown company. The stories of private Irish business owners are instructive, inspiring – and highly entertaining. We pick up and re-tell those stories informally all the time.

It struck us that gathering just some of them into a book would help the contribution of Irish entrepreneurs to be recognised as well as being an enjoyable read. Hopefully it will also give aspiring entrepreneurs encouragement, not from success stories, although all twelve of the chapters which follow are about success – but by hearing about challenges surmounted, mistakes survived and lessons learned.

Each chapter is just about as different as it could be from the next, because, rather than get in the way, we've asked each individual to tell their own story in their own distinctive voice.

We hope you gain as much enjoyment from the book as we did compiling it.

Climbing onto the Green Bandwagon

Kevin Coleman, Green Cone

The robbery happened on 4 November 1991. I was on the road with a load of products to sell wholesale, and I went into a cash-and-carry in Waterford city. They said they'd had a call from someone in my family. I was to ring home immediately.

'Something's happened to Daddy,' was my first thought, as he had not been well recently, but it was my father who answered the phone.

'Jaysus, the fright you're after giving me,' I said, sick with relief at the sound of his voice. 'I thought you were ill. Or dead.'

'I'm grand,' was his response. 'But you're not.'

He said the warehouse of our family business – run by my brother David and myself – had been broken into over the weekend. Robbed. Cleared out. It might be a good idea if I got back as soon as I could. I abandoned my schedule and headed for Dublin.

The three of us were in the business. In theory, it was me

and David, because my father, a former soccer international, had had a very slight stroke and was near retirement age anyway. David and my father had a small business selling wholesale confectionery to shops. David's been selling since he was sixteen. I haven't seen a better sales guy in my life. He would be thrown out of a place and still go back and get an order from them a day or two later.

When my father asked me to join them, I had no idea what I was getting into. It was absolutely unbelievable work – 7 in the morning until maybe 8 or 9 o'clock at night. He was the one who built it up and he did it by a fierce concentration and persistence. He never let up, never eased off. You would have to say to him at 7 p.m., 'Are you coming home tonight or what?' My brother David had the same persistence.

The cash-and-carry business was taking off in the 1980s. I went and sourced products. I got the Tayto crisps franchise and we started bringing sweets in from Spain, Germany, England and Scotland. Business took off. We got a bigger warehouse and we ended up at the top of Greenhills Road behind Xtra-vision. I always remember your man in Xtra-vision used to come down in his helicopter, and I used to think, 'Fair dues to him.'

We put vans on the road and inevitably went through a variety of performing and non-performing delivery men. David, without a doubt, was better than the best of them. He would do treble their figures, without breaking a sweat. The company was my father's; Patrick Coleman and Sons Ltd.

When he retired we called it Jolly Miller Confectionery – after a guy from Wales who bought a load of Burton's

Biscuits' old machinery and sold us biscuits by the container load.

During those good years, David and I learned one of the realities of family businesses, which is that retirement never means retirement. Even after he retired, my father would go up at lunchtime and sort out all the money and give me about twenty different little notes, like bus tickets, with instructions to do this task and that task and the other task.

'Daddy, I did that four weeks ago,' I would say, scrunching up the first note.

'Did that a fortnight back and told you about it.' Another one scrunched.

'Did this one three weeks ago' – scrunch – 'and I've forgotten how long ago I completed this last one.'

He never really pulled out of the business. He had a heart like a bull and he was a strong, strong man. At one point my four children were all under seven and three of them would get on his knee. And I'd say, 'Stop with Granddad, you'll kill him,' and he'd say, 'You leave those children alone.' A man who adored all his grandchildren.

I've no recollection of the drive back to Dublin the day the robbery was discovered. Because I had no mobile phone back then, I couldn't ask my father or my brother any of the questions rattling around in my head. Just drive. So I just drove, got to the warehouse and went in the open door. I just couldn't believe it. It was just like a vacuumed room. We were left with our shelving and that was it. Everything else gone. It was as total as if we had cleared out the warehouse in order to sell it. That empty. That naked. It echoed when you walked around it.

We had finished work on the Saturday about 12. I'd gone home at lunchtime and, as normal, I brought my two boys down to the rugby club to watch a match. Apparently, the robbers moved in on Saturday afternoon, staying until they were finished. They stole our big delivery lorry as well as using their own transport. When David went in on the Monday, the sensors and bells were off the wall on the floor. The phone lines were cut. Customers had telephoned over the weekend, we discovered later, to leave messages, but when they got no signal they just thought it was a fault. It would never have occurred to a casual caller that a highly organised crime was going on and that the lack of a phone signal was a consequence of that. The gang cut the lines to the whole industrial estate, not just us.

We were not an easy target, that was the irony of it. We had always taken security very seriously, even when we were mainly dealing with confectionery, but once you get into bulk cigarettes, security becomes a key aspect of your business. Early on, we had a safe we had bought from an ammunition company in Knocklyon many moons ago. Fort Knox for cigarettes.

When we got bigger we got another one made, exactly like it. I remember walking through the big cavernous cleaned-out warehouse that Monday to see if they'd tackled the safe. The rest of the operation was so professionally done, I figured they had.

They had. It looked like a tin savings box that someone had attacked with a can opener. What was curious was that there were seats all around. A semi circle of seats around the distorted metal of the safe, as if they'd held a meeting. Scattered around each chair were cigarette butts. Several per chair. Several per man. They'd obviously been smoking like chimneys while they worked out how to get at the hundreds of thousands of cigarettes behind the steel door. It looked for all the world as if five guys had been sitting looking at the safe and discussing how they were going to get into this thing. Brute force was the short answer. Brute force and a lot of it.

They broke the top left-hand corner and doubled it back over with some sort of gear or a large iron pole or something. They took every cigarette we had. Thousands and thousands and thousands of cigarettes – of every brand and nature. The three of us did that pointless thing you do when an unprecedented disaster strikes: play the 'what if?' game. What if my father, as he so often did, had decided to go in over the weekend just to check on something? What if one of us had been passing, happened to see their lights and lorries and decided to investigate?

We were lucky none of the 'what if' possibilities had happened. That was about the only luck we had. We were alive and well and product-free. Not a packet of fags left.

The insurance company wouldn't believe the figures we gave them. They kept asking for more details. For confirmation. For paperwork. Meanwhile, we had nothing to sell and nothing to buy anything with. Six months down the line I told them I was bringing them to court.

'You can't have it every way,' I told them. 'You took the money from us in a hefty premium. We got done, and now you won't pay out. We're going under. What the hell are ye at? What do you think we are? Let me tell you, we had a few break-ins all right, or attempted break-ins, but we hadn't

GALWAY COUNTY LIBRARIES

claimed because our no-claims status would have been gone and ye'd have jacked up the premium – and now, when we get done by an organised gang, you're messing and postponing? We'll see ye in court.'

On the steps of the court they settled. We got all the money. That was the good news. We could go back into business. The bad news was that we could go back into business only if we paid an annual insurance premium of £40,000, which was double what we'd been paying before the robbery. And they put an excess of £40,000 on our policy.

'We're going to pay them £40,000 and then if we get robbed again, we have to cover the first £40,000 of the loss ourselves?' I said. 'I don't think so. I really don't think so. That's crazy.'

I was tired, physically and mentally. I couldn't believe that all we'd put into the business didn't count, after the robbery. It was just number-crunching and out came a premium amount that would have crippled us. Having built up a business that had literally started in our own home. In the beginning, when we got into cigarettes, what we would do is buy 100,000 John Player Blue. Because of the size of the order, we would get 20,000 free. So 20,000 was our profit; we sold them at cost. But since we didn't have a warehouse at the time, we stuffed all these John Player Blue into the house in Rathfarnham. They were piled high in the bedrooms. They were like extra walls in the garage. The only room John Player Blue didn't invade was my parents' bedroom. The whole house reeked of tobacco, in spite of the wrapping around the cartons and the packages. My poor mother's home – for a while – was transformed into a stinky warehouse.

After all that, after my years on the road with product, after David's marvellous salesmanship, we were being asked to start all over again like three convicts in the *Dandy*, dragging a heavy weight attached to our ankles. It just wasn't on. So we just closed it down and we settled with all the companies we owed money to.

I had no idea what I was going to do next. I'd never had one of those career plans blocked out in five-year segments. When I started working in Smurfits directly having sat my Leaving Cert, the nearest I had to a plan was to go back to school – Terenure College – because I was underage for rugby and I played for Leinster schools.

'Next year is the first year of Irish schools and you've a good chance,' I told myself.

But I got the job, took the job, took the money. I went into the sales office, answering phones and getting orders, collecting them and having them ready, dealing with people in the showrooms and running around like a rabbit. I enjoyed it and after about six months I bought a car. My father gave me a loan of £270 to buy a Fiat 850 – that was really something in those days. I made £18 a week and I paid him £7; it was a fiver for juice and I'd six quid left – happy days!

I got picked for the Leinster under-19 team at seventeen and my boss, Tim Duggan, gave me a lot of time off. We played in London, and against Llanelli. The under-19 team had five of the international players later on – John Robbie, Ian Burns, Tony Ward, Frank Ennis and Rodney O'Donnell. John Robbie was a super guy, super-intelligent. I got on very well with him. I played two seasons with Leinster under-19.

I was on the road for four years working for Smurfits, selling stationery and office equipment. I remember one day driving from Ballymount to the old Smurfit building in Santry, where Michael Smurfit was based, with the refill for his Parker pen. His secretary could have got it across the road in the shop, but I didn't mind doing it. I knew I'd get the mileage money for the journey.

I bought a house when I was nineteen – my mother made me do it. It was in Dargle Wood in Knocklyon, a four-bed-room house for £14,950. That's the thing about making a lot of money as a salesman – you have to put it away, rather than sink it all into drinking pints on the road with other reps. My mother was a very switched-on lady.

So although I never had a career plan, I'd had a great career before joining David and my father in business. Not just in Smurfits, but in other companies after I left Smurfits. I never had to apply for a job. I was always head-hunted. Not just head-hunted, but head-hunted by people I liked. I have always been very lucky with people. I was married and had a family I adored.

After we closed down the business, as a result of the rob-bery, David went on in a much smaller way for a while, and I tried various jobs, including working for an English company in Ireland, setting up and directing their sales team. But I was beginning to tire of working for other people.

The opportunity presented itself when my mother died, and I was left a few bob.

'I'm going to look for something to do on my own,' I decided. I had a friend over in Toronto – Greg Ward and his wife – he invited me to go over for a couple of weeks. I was delighted to accept the invitation, although when the plane stopped at Shannon I was already so homesick for the family that if I could have got a plane back to Dublin I would have abandoned the trip and headed straight back.

Greg's job was as a salesman for Avery labels, Canada, in one of these retail nurseries like Homebase. That was how I first saw the Green Cone, a natural food digester. Very impressive. Great possibilities. I thought about it a lot. Greg was working and then in the evening we'd have a barbecue. I'd be talking about the Green Cone and Greg would be talking about me emigrating and going to work with him in Toronto, which was an attractive possibility, if it wasn't for the fact that I found Toronto people to be extremely rude and the traffic was mind-boggling. The 401 interstate went from Toronto up to Buffalo Niagara Falls – and there are four lanes on each side. Always filled with thousands of cars. One particular Friday we said we'd go off early and go for a few pints to the Irish pub. From the time we left to the time we arrived at the pub was four hours, and I said, 'No, no. There's no way I'm putting up with that.'

So I came home, but the Canadian trip had been incredibly productive, because of discovering the Green Cone. I was totally sold on it.

The Green Cone is made up of four injection-moulded plastic sections. A basket is installed below. Above ground there's a black inner cone and a green outer lidded plastic cone. The diameter of the outer Green Cone is 59cm at its base and 28cm at the lid end, and the Green Cone stands less than 70cm above the ground.

What it does is eat everything you don't. Or that your family doesn't. That means all household waste, including raw or cooked meat, fish, bones, vegetable peelings, apple cores, tea bags, bread crusts. It comes with a neat little kitchen caddy so householders can turf their kitchen waste into it and carry it out to the Green Cone, having sprinkled a little accelerator powder (included on purchase) on it.

The Green Cone works through solar heating. Heat builds up between the inner and outer cones. Beneficial micro-organisms grow and start an aerobic digestion process that breaks everything down into water, carbon dioxide and a tiny amount of undigested material – only enough to require removal every few years. You position it somewhere in the garden where there's a bit of sunshine, and the liquid that comes out into the ground underneath is so rich in nutrients, the surrounding plants become so lush and verdant, it's amazing. It's as if they're being fertilised every day – except that this nutrient-rich liquid is free and saves the money you'd be paying for a wheelie bin filled with food waste which would then go to one of our overflowing landfill sites. It's neat. It's environmental and it's simple. It's low maintenance. It's cheap – less than €180. It lasts forever.

Canada had fallen in love with it. The makers would set up a marquee in a shopping centre car park and sell literally thousands of units on a Saturday afternoon. Local author-ities invested heavily in the Green Cone, because it reduced pressure on landfills and incinerators. Given Ireland's obsession with landfills and incinerators and our nat-ional move towards more environmentally-friendly waste disposal, it was a no-brainer that the Green Cone would be a hit here, too.

I didn't do any sophisticated market research or anything. The first thing I did was get one for myself, to test it out and see if it really worked as well as the websites claimed. If anything, it worked better. I ended up calling my local authority and asking them to take away my wheelie bin because I simply stopped using it. I rang them several times and each time they promised they would, but they never did. I have one redundant wheelie bin at home. Maybe they don't get that many requests for their removal. GALWAY COUNTY LIBRARIES

'This thing is a flier,' I thought. 'I'll be a millionaire in no time.' As it turned out, that was a bit optimistic.

I got the franchise for Ireland and hit the road, because I figured local authorities were the first bulk market. They had to want to supply every householder in their area with these things, to reduce waste collections, the cost of waste collections, the cost of landfill maintenance and all that bad stuff, right? Wrong. 185.589

The one thing I had not factored in was that many of the local authorities had tied themselves to contracts with waste-removal companies. They had outsourced the function to those contractors, and if they were now to install Green Cones in everybody's garden, the amount of waste to be collected by those contractors would drop like a stone, and the contractors would get litigious, claiming that the local authority was subverting the agreed contract. So, in one county after another, I met with genuine enthusiasm from experts who could see the benefits of the Green Cone, but no action, because of the existing contracts with waste-removing firms.

I did get Cavan, Louth and Meath. Mayo bought some as well, as did community schools around the country. But my initial high hopes of bulk sales didn't materialise, which made me very glad that I had not set up a major company with a rake of employees. If I had done it that way – the traditional way – I would have been in trouble, whereas because I had invested my own time and mileage, all I had to do was re-group and reduce my expectations of the market. I realised I had to target individuals. That meant leaflet drops.

In the beginning I did those drops myself, pushing as many as 500 attractive cone shaped leaflets in through letterboxes. I'd never really thought about letterboxes before, but once you're doing personal leaflet drops you really think about letterboxes and how oddly they are positioned on many houses.

'Why do some people have letterboxes you can't find?' I'd be asking myself, ploughing around the front of a house trying to figure where – logically – the owners might have chosen to site their mailbox.

The leaflets paid off. The calls started to come in from individual potential customers. It started to get busy. I couldn't deliver the cones personally as it would have cost a fortune; so in the beginning I was FastTracking the Green Cones and paying for them up front. Then I got a call from a company called Fastway Couriers.

'We can't do it any more. The Green Cones are too big for our small vans. We're not making any money.' They were totally up front about it, which was fair enough.

So I asked a very good friend of mine, Derek Webster, who was in the transport business, if he knew anyone who would deliver them. 'I will,' was his response. 'I'll warehouse them for you and I'll deliver them.'

These cones come on pallets of thirty, with the boxes underneath. Derek's company doesn't charge me for warehouse, they charge me €2 for putting them together and into the box, and then they charge me per-cone delivery.

The big companies haven't bitten yet. I'll try to get a deal with them – if a big company will allow me to deliver just to one spot, we could send them in on the pallets, which would save me a fortune, and I could give a reduction. We've got a few companies to bite, a few co-ops, and the councils.

I started the business selling Green Cones about four or five years ago, and progress was patchy for several years. But I never doubted that they would work, never doubted that there was a market for them, never doubted that eventually, every house in this country will have one, and every business and public facility will have several. It's lucky that I have this unquenchable belief in the product, because the setbacks have been gruesome.

For example, early on, when it was clear that county councils were not going to fall over themselves to buy a few thousand apiece, I gave consideration to selling the Green Cone through nurseries and DIY shops, but the mathematics didn't make sense. The margin on the product wouldn't allow me to make any profit that way.

'Right,' I thought. 'I'm on my own. I'll do it my own way.' Doing it my own way started with the leaflet drops and moved on to the website. We won a competition for direct marketing. We have a mentor coming in from the South Dublin Enterprise Board – Liam Burkett, a St Mary's man. Then there are the newsletters – I get a lot of information into the *Southside People*, the *Northside People* and all those sorts of papers. At one point, I paid the *Southside People* to drop 40,000 leaflets.

Declan Egan is my accountant. He was a year older than me in school and he said to me, 'Is there any chance of getting part of the action?' I said, 'What would you like to get out of it?' and he said he'd do all the books and everything as part of his involvement. If I was making a few bob then he'd make a few bob. And I said, 'That's perfectly fine by me.' I have a very informal way of doing business. It's the only way I know how to do it. We're all going to end up in a box, and there's nobody better than me, nobody worse than I am.

I'm not a marketing man, I'm a salesman. I present something to someone and they might say, 'I'll think about it,' and I'd say, 'Is there any question I haven't answered, because if you've to think about it, I haven't convinced you.' That's the way I go about it. I wouldn't bully anybody.

In the beginning, I couldn't afford any advertising for the Green Cone, but every newspaper was written to and I went down to community centres and gave talks, and spoke to any environmental groups having a compost day. Word spread and they would ring me and say, 'Will you come down?' I remember driving to Newport, Co. Mayo, one night the Irish soccer team were playing and I thought there wouldn't be a sinner in the place because the match was on. But the place was full. I sold loads of them.

Recently, I've been investing on a very small scale in advertising. I took out half-page ads in directories in Cork, in four different areas. I'm getting orders because it's on the front page of the telephone directory. When I get the directories I send fifty to sixty businesses a letter about the Green Cone and say, 'I would be obliged if you would put it on your notice board.' I've got a lot of referrals that way.

Just as I couldn't afford an ad agency, I couldn't afford a public relations agency either. I wrote to radio and TV programmes, sent them leaflets about the Green Cone and followed up with telephone calls. I really, really wanted to get the Green Cone onto Duncan Stewart's programme, but I was getting nowhere with them.

Then, one day I was up around Nassau Street in Dublin and there was Duncan Stewart filming an item about the new bins and green waste. I was there like everybody else having a look, and I said to myself, 'Well, here's the man.' I went over to him between filming. 'Would you mind if I had a word with you when you're finished?' I asked him. 'I'll stay over there on the left.'

In fairness, when he had his piece to camera done, he came over, and I told him about the Green Cone. When I told him the huge sales figures in different countries, he became very interested.

'Could you get one of these to my office?'

'Of course I could.'

That was about 11 a.m. I had a Green Cone assembled and everything in his office at 2 p.m. He rang me back within minutes. 'We're filming in Waterford in six days, would you put a Green Cone into a garden between now and next Wednesday?'

I said I'd go down first thing Monday morning and do it. I installed the thing with my bare hands, because I wrongly assumed a) the householder would be there when I arrived and b) that they'd have a shovel. They weren't and they didn't, so I dug the hole for the base of the Green Cone using my hands. My hands didn't look great for a couple of days, but it was worth it. It was so worth it.

They did the filming for RTÉ's *Eco-Eye* and Duncan interviewed me. I'd never been on television before and I'd never been trained, so I was extremely nervous and bothered, afterwards, that I had been rubbish. When it went out, though, I was told I was brilliant. The slagging I got was fantastic. I watched it at home and all the family were ringing me up. All the lads heard about it and they were calling me 'The Green Coneman' and all this sort of stuff.

We've a sales target of a hundred a month and we've beaten that target every time. The monthly sales are rising. It was a natural progression to research something bigger because I was thinking, 'This is great, but it can't be used in a hotel or a restaurant, because it can't cope with the volumes of food waste generated by a place like that.' So I was looking to see if there was anything else in the market that would digest commercial or industrial waste.

I spent hours on the internet. Then, bingo! The Green Rocket. The Green Rocket from Warrington in England. I contacted the company – a father and son operation – and told them I was interested in selling their machine in Ireland. I got the next flight over and we did a deal. He was an absolute gent, and his son was too. We've sold the Green Rocket to hotels, restaurants and the prison service – Castlerea prison has one. A Carmelite order in Ballinteer has one. They're stainless steel and they look like a coffin on a stand. There are three models: a half-tonne, one-tonne or two-tonne capacity per week. We give an industrial shredder with it, so say, for example, you've a bit of a tree – put it into the shredder and boom! Food waste creates nitrogen and you've got to counteract that with carbon, which is wood or wood derivatives. I give a three-year guarantee – parts, service or whatever. In addition, I go down and train the staff myself.

What's left in the digesters is an earthy compost. It's top grade. They use it in the United States by putting an additive in it and spreading it on the greens on golf courses. In a lot of the golf clubs here, though, the problem is that the catering is farmed out and the golf club just pays the bills. However, I'll find a way around that sooner or later.

I'm always on the search for more products. When you're the head of such a small company, commitment to customer service is absolute. It has to be. I do make mistakes – don't get me wrong, I've made mistakes in deliveries and I will put my hands up and say so. At the end of the day it's my fault because I'm head of the company. About two months ago we were six Green Cones short for deliveries and I had to call six people and say, 'Listen, my fault.' I don't leave people short. I work bloody hard at this. I'm not going to let it go, and eventually it's going to take off in a big way.

I'm not an environmentalist, but the business I'm in makes

you more environmentally aware. I bring all my bottles for recycling – before, everything went into the bin – and I use the green bin for all the paper and cardboard, like everybody else.

When I researched more I found the Green Earthmaker. It's from New Zealand. When I found it, I said, 'This is the best thing since sliced bread.' Because it works by gravity, you have compost in half the time. It's a superb product but it is expensive. You can put your grass, your hedge clippings, twigs, old plants in it; you can shred paper in it, you can put in some shredded cardboard. You can put uncooked peelings and fruit in.

I haven't made a million and I don't have guys knocking on my door making me an offer for the franchise, but I know somebody is going to make a hell of a lot of money out of this, and I hope it's going to be me. I'll give myself another nine years – I'll be sixty.

I don't believe I would have achieved any success without the backing of my parents, brothers and sister. My father, without a doubt, gave me the best bit of advice I ever got. He said, 'It's just as easy to be courteous as it is to be rude.' I don't care if it's Michael Smurfit or Joe Bloggs, I would be as courteous to one as to the other. In fact, I would probably be more courteous to Joe Bloggs. That's important, because in my career and in my life I've dealt with people who are not very nice people. But I was always nice.

When I think of myself, even now, I don't think 'entrepreneur' or 'businessman' – it's always 'salesman'. You can't beat the buzz. Even an order on the phone. You can't beat the buzz of selling …

Breakfast, Lunch and Dinner

Pat Walsh, Walsh Mushrooms

I was brought up in a family general stores in a small village, Knocklong, Co. Limerick. It had grocery, drapery, bakery, animal feed, coal and a timber yard. It was the days of 'half days' and every Thursday after school, as kids, we had to make up bags of sugar and tea for the busy Friday and Saturday. So I had my first commercial and entrepreneurial experience engendered from an early age from my parents, serving behind the counter when I could hardly see over it.

I was sent away to boarding school in Castleknock, Dublin and then studied horticulture in UCC for two years before spending a year on practical horticulture in Holland prior to coming back and getting a job as horticulturist just about the time that Erin Foods was starting up.

I was second-last of a family of ten and it was getting to be a bit of a struggle for my mother to put us all through college. I was a bit of a waster at college anyway, enjoying my first escape from rural or institutional confinement.

But I got the job with Erin Foods, going around advising farmers. Erin Foods was trying to get farmers to grow carrots and peas and other vegetables. I'd go around with one of the more senior agricultural advisors who had these beet contract signing meetings. We had a sort of a 'slush fund' to buy the farmers a few pints and persuade them to plant a few acres of carrots and peas beside their twenty or thirty acres of beet.

The Sugar Company then was a semi-state body. General Costello, the chief executive of the Sugar Company at the time, had this great ambition that Ireland would be a food island, hence the decision to set up Erin Foods. Unfortunately, they chose to go processed when the UK was starting to move towards fresh produce. Nonetheless, in common with many people that you'll find in the Irish food industry today, I got my adult business education in Erin Foods.

I was only a few months in the job when Erin Foods decided to get into mushrooms. They decided they wanted to grow mushrooms for the soups they were making. So when they wanted to get somebody to go and learn about mushroom growing, I was the only one in the company who spoke Dutch, and for that I was sent back to Holland for another three or four months. In those days Erin Foods had a very particular corporate culture. General Costello was an ex-army man. You weren't asked what you'd like to do, you were just told.

I actually spoke Dutch very well, and had an old motor-bike, which I had bought having worked a summer in the UK canneries. We were down in Zeeland in the south-west – same location as Kerry in Ireland – and we were quite near the estuary going up to Antwerp, so, frequently, after the day's work on the farm we would all head down and go for a swim. We came out after a swim one evening and here was a cop standing beside my motorbike, which of course had no tax on it.

And because I was in my working overalls having been on the farm, I certainly hadn't a passport or a driver's licence on me so we went through the whole rigmarole. Anyways, he pulled out the ticket book and gave me a ticket for having no tax on my motorbike. It only struck me after he was gone that he clearly did not accept that I was a foreigner and a visitor. I talked colloquial Dutch well enough to give the impression I was a native – and got fined as a reward.

The Dutch were quite advanced in the industry and actually ran a school attached to the research station then. It's a very big industry. These days, they produce about 250,000 tonnes per year. Ireland would produce about 80,000 tonnes, which isn't bad.

When I came back, Erin Foods started a mushroom farm in the grounds of the sugar factory in Thurles. The General was very proud of the fact that they could do virtually everything in-house. There was no such thing as bringing in big outside contractors or anything. One of the engineers designed the buildings and I ordered the equipment.

We had a cannery, drying plant and mushroom farm and perhaps eighty people working in the operation. At the proud old age of twenty-two or twenty-three, I was in charge of an interesting and complex operation. I was holding down the kind of job that you wouldn't get until you were forty nowadays. In addition, I was part of something new, something adventurous. It was very ambitious of the General to set up a food industry when there were no skills in the country to manage it. That risk-taking meant that lots of young people like myself were given great opportunities. For that, I'll always be grateful.

We weren't the first mushroom farm in Ireland. There were in fact a couple of substantial farms and they were rather concerned about a state company coming into business. One was in Co. Cork and the other in Co. Kildare which was started in Nissen huts, used as dormitories for migratory workers harvesting turf during and after the Second World War.

But then after a few years, even though I was enjoying what I was doing, I decided to move on. The semi-state culture didn't particularly appeal to me; I felt I had a little bit more in me. I moved onto another small operation with a few local guys and we started a small mushroom farm in Co. Tipperary. This only lasted a couple of years. It was really small and it was struggling. Then the place actually went on fire and that was the end of it. I should point out that I was away when the fire started, so I have a good alibi.

Those were bad times. I moved back in with my mother in Co. Limerick and returned to milking the cows. It was pretty tough for six or twelve months. Fortunately, things began to look up again.

I was approached by an ex-Erin Foods man, Seamus MacGiolla Riagh, who wanted to start a mushroom farm up in Gorey, and that's how I came to move to Co. Wexford in 1969. I had only been married a year when I went there, literally into a green field, and had to use the engineering skills I had learned building the Erin Foods mushroom farm.

I took a very small share, minute rather than small, because

I didn't have the price of anything at that particular stage. Just to get a job was a tremendous relief. We got it up and running by 1970, which wasn't bad, having only turned the sod at the end of 1969. It went very well for the first few years – so much so that in 1974 we decided to triple the size of it. This coincided with the first oil crisis. We used huge quantities of oil for heating purposes, and suddenly the oil went up threefold. The present oil crisis is nothing by comparison.

Most of the mushroom farms at the time were what you might call 'factory farms'. They did everything. They made compost, they grew the mushrooms and they sold the mushrooms themselves. It was labour-intensive. What I had seen in Holland wasn't like that. The industry was organised on a different basis. The compost was made centrally and it was sold out to smaller growers who just grew mushrooms. And they in turn would go back to the cooperative to sell their produce. These thoughts, these comparisons were circling in my head during the bad years following the 1974 oil crisis.

We needed to have scale in the composting operation to sell the compost to smaller growers who were, effectively, a cottage industry. They would have more control over the labour-intensive aspect of it. Particularly an operation like growing mushrooms, which is like milking cows: an everyday-of-the-week operation and usually that's better off done in the small family unit.

It was actually 1979 before I left the Gorey operation and then only moved a few miles away. It wasn't a big strategic decision about where to move. We were settled in Gorey by this time and we now had three kids. I mentioned to my wife

GALWAY COUNTY LIBRARIES

that I was thinking of locating here or there. 'I don't care where you're locating,' she told me. 'I'm staying here.'

So Gorey it was. I got a site the other side of town and started off. We had to persuade people to get into mushroom growing and build houses for it. It was hard work and, God be good to him, John Daly, who was chief agriculture officer in Co. Wexford at the time, was a great help to me. He came to parish meetings and persuaded growers by his sheer belief in the concept. But it was a hell of a struggle at times.

We started off with the princely number of seven growers. The one asset I did have arose from me going back to my mother and persuading her – probably against her better judgement – to sell the farm in Limerick, which provided me with a good lump of cash. I told her that I would support her thereafter. I was quite nervous myself so I put half of the money into the mushroom business and put the other half in a transport business and I have to say the mushroom business was worth a damn sight more than the transport business as it turned out.

The mushrooms took off. It was very small in the beginning, a real struggle. But after a few years the concept got going. There was no point in getting people to grow mushrooms without providing some marketing expertise for them. We wouldn't have the population to take them. So exports started in a tiny way: a transit van collecting from the seven growers and hitting the ferry in Rosslare to get to Cardiff for first thing in the morning and the market there. It opened at five in the morning, the same as the Dublin fruit market. That's how we got going.

Our satellite approach proved to be much more efficient than the old factory farm. We were a few years in business and growing very slowly when the big old factory farm in Gorey that I'd worked in went into receivership and we bought it. That would have been in the mid-1980s. We bought the place from the receiver, Hugh Cooney. He was young at the time, although he probably aged ten years during the six months he spent running the operation. He went in there as the receiver in the springtime. Summer is a particularly difficult time in the mushroom industry – and, of course, that was precisely the time we were thinking about buying it. But by the end of the summer we took the plunge and made the purchase.

We didn't go back in and start running a factory farm, but instead turned it into the type of operation we already had. We just made the compost. We went and talked to the former employees and they rented the growing houses and became the growers, running their own businesses.

Our growth was greatly helped by the collapse of other traditional factory farm operations. Perhaps six months or so after that farm in Gorey went into receivership, a big one in Kildare – Carbury – went into receivership and I obviously took an interest in that. Cathal McCanne, who was head of mushroom research in what is now Teagasc, persuaded a couple of English friends and myself into a joint venture and he became the managing director.

We did the very same in Carbury as we'd done in Gorey: privatised the houses and said to former employees, 'if you want to grow mushrooms, hire the houses; we'll make the compost for you, and sell the mushrooms for you.'

In fairness, I should acknowledge the fact that Carbury, being a successful business over the years, would have grown about three or four times in size from the original 'Nissen huts'. It was a big operation, acres of huts and piles of compost.

Not long afterwards, a big factory farm in England came on the market and we ended up buying it as well. Times were good. We had now made it. We had got to the stage where the system was working well, delivering the volume we needed. It was at that point I realised that whenever things were going really well, one or two things would always go horribly wrong. Either the exchange rate of the Irish pound to sterling would wobble the wrong way, or something would go wrong with the compost – some virus would strike.

When the punt separated from sterling, it actually went to a premium and we were getting creamed. We were suffering a higher cost of production and – to complicate the costs – having to ship to the UK. It was a horrific time. All we could do was hang in and hope it turned around. The IDA gave us some help, but this got the English industry up in arms and heading off to Brussels to get a ruling about such aid being anti-competitive. We would end up having to give it back but at least we got it when we needed it, and when the exchange rate changed to a more favourable level we could afford to give it back.

The industry grew hugely during the 1980s and early 1990s, peaking at about 1,000 growers. It was labour intensive, suited to an Irish economic climate of 18 to 20 per cent interest rates, which was horrific, but cheap labour. The 'Celtic Tiger' economy, with low interest rates and expensive labour, brought new challenges and the industry rationalised down to less than one hundred modern well-mechanised farms, which produce as much as the previous 1,000.

We sold our joint venture interest, as we were having some conflicts of interest in the market place, and concentrated our resources on building new well-mechanised compost facilities to serve the new breed of growers.

The country grows about 80,000 tonnes and only consumes about 20,000 tonnes. Three quarters of what is produced is exported to the UK, where it meets stiff competition from Holland and Poland. Poland's advantage is that its agricultural wages are less than €2 an hour, whereas we're on €8 an hour for harvesting, which is still done by hand.

So we have had ups and downs and radical change, but are still surviving after twenty-seven years. I am semi-retired now and just look in to keep an eye on the compost-making, which is very subjective. It helps to keep management's eye on the ball.

Mushrooms will always be in demand. Somebody once described the mushroom as the third most consumed vegetable in the world. Mushrooms are ubiquitous. You get them in salads and you get them in soups. They are nearly everywhere except in desserts. You can have them for breakfast. They are one of the few things you can have for breakfast, lunch and dinner.

If You Can Dream It, You Can Become It

Sean Gallagher, Smarthomes

A couple of years ago, I went looking for the man who had given me sight. I didn't know if he was alive or dead. All I knew was his name, Dr Thompkins, that he'd worked in the Royal Victoria Eye and Ear hospital when I was a child, and that I remembered him, with gratitude, every single morning of my life.

I was born with congenital cataracts. Forty-five years ago, that meant you were virtually blind, and there was no treatment. For the first three years of my life I couldn't see better than if I'd been looking through the thick bottom of a glass bottle. Then I ended up in the care of this surgeon in the Eye and Ear. He did an operation on my eyes that was somewhere between experiment and art. It was delicate. It was dangerous. I've never found anybody else who had it done. It made the crucial difference to my life. Not just because it gave me sight, but because it gave me the beginning of belonging.

I could see now but not as well as others around me.

When you're different in school, you get treated differently. Maybe not so badly now as in the past, but a disability like a visual impairment can isolate you. A teacher in a primary school these days who encounters a kid with a visual impairment would probably refer them to a specialist. Back then, and probably not knowing any better, what they did was put me in the dunce's class. Because I could only see words and not see full sentences, I read slowly and awkwardly. They presumed that I was not bright. That's why, nearly half a century later, I went looking for the surgeon – now ninety years of age – to say 'thank you'.

The other person I'm indebted to was a teacher, Tom Gawley, who, when I was in sixth class in school, pulled me aside after a drama class.

'Sean, you have talents you don't know you have,' he said to me. 'The only thing you're missing is the confidence to follow them. You may not take the same path other people take, but you need to find your own talent. You can be anything you want to be, so long as you can dream it. If you can dream it, you can become it.'

Those two men gave me a sense of possibility that I started to deliver on in my teens. I set up the first youth club in my home town in 1979, coming back on the bus from the Pope's visit. I discovered that there are needs everywhere and if there was a gap somewhere, wherever it was, you should fill it. So I set up the first youth club and embarked then on a personal development programme, based on the words of my teacher: 'If you can dream it, you can become it.' During the personal development programme, I sat down and wrote out five things.

It was valuable to me, because it forced me beyond the vagueness of a lot of people who want to be an entrepreneur but who don't have an idea. They're like someone turning up at the Olympics – all confidence, fitness and dressed in the right gear – who just don't know what event they're in.

Writing my life plan at eighteen, I had the disadvantage of not having a college degree, but the advantage of unconditional support from my parents.

'Sean, whatever you do, we don't have any concerns that you're going to be successful at it,' they used to say to me. 'And whatever you choose to do now, you may not do for the rest of your life. But you'll be successful at it, one way or the other.'

The first of the five ambitions I wrote into the life plan came from the fact that I'd always liked agriculture and the outdoor life. I liked physical hard work.

'I want to be a farmer,' I wrote down. 'That's number one.'

Secondly, I'd been working in youth clubs.

'I want to be in youth work,' I wrote next. 'Particularly with people who've come through their own personal challenges.'

The third pillar was that, because I liked sport, I wanted to be a martial artist. The fourth was that, arising out of my interest in youth work, I wanted to be in politics. The last thing I put down was that I wanted to start my own business because I loved some of the local business guys, loved the buzz around them and the wheeling and dealing.

In 1980, with my Leaving Cert out of the way, I went to the local agricultural college for a year and soon after that got my first full time job working in sales for Bailieborough Co-op. In 1983, I bought a farm and I was on the way. But I had no money to buy animals, so what I did was identify a need among old farmers to have sheds and outhouses painted. I would paint them at the weekends, and instead of charging them money, I would get them to give me a calf as payment. Over the course of a summer, I would paint eight or ten farmers' places, and get eight or ten calves. I was getting the feed cheap from the Co-op. I was learning about cost, overheads, cashflow and – most of all – about sweat equity.

Then, one morning around 8.30, I was driving to put bales of hay out for the animals, when another car came around the corner on my side of the road and collided with mine. I sustained neck and back injuries that put me out of action, physically, for about eighteen months – lying on the floor to cope with the pain.

'Hold on, I have a challenge here,' I told myself. 'Physio isn't working. Have to try something else.'

I got into health and fitness and exercise. Took up judo. Took up massage training. Found out how to stretch muscles and make my body work again. I was now back on track. And then I went to Maynooth on a two-year course in youth work, the first of its kind, and got my diploma in youth and community development. It's now a degree course, covering everything from psychology and group work to facilitation skills.

Out of that, the following year, I was commissioned to write the government's first alcohol education programme. I spent two years on that, while also working with young offenders and speaking at conferences on youth-related issues. Then Dr Rory O'Hanlon, the Fianna Fáil TD and Minister for Health at that time, asked me to become his political secretary. I spent a couple of years working in the Dáil for Rory. It was a great time, because of the sense of being at the centre of things, the ability to get things done, to address people's priorities and concerns, to be effective. The great buzz of politics comes from belonging to something more important than yourself – a fundamental human need I had learned about earlier in Maslow's hierarchy of needs.

The personal fulfilment attached to politics can't be denied, although it can be a tough life. Rory, as Minister for Health at a time of cutbacks, came in for enormous abuse from the opposition because of hospitals closing down at the time. He is a man of enormous integrity and loyalty. He believed in collective cabinet responsibility. And as part of a cabinet that made tough decisions, he believed he had to take whatever stick came from doing the job he had to do in the interests of the country, even if he had to pay the price of diminished personal popularity. I came to respect him greatly as a politician and as a friend.

I had a network of contacts built up within departments so good that other ministers would ring me to get things done. I just knew my way around the system. The first people I spoke to when I went into a government department were the guys at the gate. Why? Because they were the guys who opened up in the morning and shut the place down at night and you had to get in and out. The people in the restaurant, similarly, were the people who fed you. And they deserved exactly the same respect as a department secretary general or a minister. The more you do for people – just because it's the right thing to do, not out of any cute hoorism – the better network you have and the better your chances that they'd help you out if you were in difficulty. I could ring someone in a government department and say, 'There's a case file somewhere, at the bottom of such and such a drawer, is there any chance you'd look it up for me?' and they would because there were no bully-boy tactics involved. It wasn't about sending strong letters.

The political pendulum has swung to such a degree in the intervening years that if you do a favour for someone it's assumed there's something sleazy behind it. That's unfair. If you think about it, good business is all about relationships. Business people and customers don't buy from businesses. They buy from people. Companies don't start businesses. Individuals start businesses. It's all about personal relationships, rapport, motivation. For me, in business as in politics, that's what it's all about: relationship-building.

During that time I got actively immersed and involved in Ógra Fianna Fáil and within a period of a year or so had become head of the youth wing of the party nationally, also securing membership of the party's illustrious national executive. I was passionate about politics and this was an electric time. But politics has its downsides, as I was soon to learn.

The insecurity, the precariousness of political life hit home when Albert Reynolds took over as Fianna Fáil leader and did an Andrews Liver Salts purge of his cabinet. Rory was to lose his post and so was I. Within hours we were gone, our desks cleared and some new lessons learned. I went for a short time into Fianna Fáil HQ, but that wasn't where I wanted to be at the time. I missed the cut and thrust and the buzz of the front line.

Then I got a great opportunity from Noel Dempsey, TD,

to tackle a reorganisation of county councillors. Dempsey was a very personable guy with no airs or graces or political trappings. He was part of a new Fianna Fáil and a man I had come to admire greatly. He probably knew I could get along with the young guy who'd just been elected, in his twenties, to the council for the first time, and the old guy who had spent forty years there and had little hunger for change, and move both into the modern age of technology, communications and public speaking.

'Could you go away and think about a proposal or some idea about how we could structure an approach to modernising the role of the county councillor in Irish politics?' he asked me.

I went back to him with the plan and he offered me the job. I was due to start on the Monday. I had my desk picked out and all. It was a job that I knew I would love, that I knew I could do well and one that I believed needed to be done.

Then came a phone call from Co. Louth to say that there was a job on offer with the County Enterprise Board, to come up and stimulate enterprise and new business development within Louth and the border area. I reverted to my original plan, to set up my own enterprise.

Then came some realisations: 'One, I don't have the business idea,' I said to myself. 'Two, I really haven't amassed a huge amount of business acumen and I have no formal training. So if I'm looking for a bridge between politics and business, the Enterprise Board seems perfect. I can delve into a whole variety of businesses, assess business plans, give out money and run 'start your own business' programmes. I can get experience, and while I'm getting it the idea will come along.'

I left Dublin in 1995 and went to Dundalk, which wasn't a big transition for me because, as a Cavan man, I was familiar with the border area. My five-year plan was to soak up everything I could, go back to college and get my MBA and then set up my own business. And that's exactly what I did.

I got married in the middle of it. I met someone through doing the MBA who was lovely, had personality, had similar interests, had a great intellect. In those three years I got engaged, married and separated. And learned something about the need for work/life balance, but I'll come back to that.

In 1997, as part of the County Enterprise Board, I led a trade mission of small companies from the border area to the east coast of the United States. I got talking to a young guy in a small engineering company, Derek Roddy from outside Dundalk. The two of us had just bought new houses, and we realised that the extent of the technological infrastructure in our new houses was a telephone socket in the hall.

The two of us mirrored what was happening everywhere at the time. Within a month or so of moving in, the new owners wanted a TV, so they put the dish up and got a hole drilled through a good wall to let the cables through. Then they'd want a telephone extension in the bedroom, and lumps of skirting board would come off to accommodate the cable.

'This isn't just us,' Derek Roddy said to me. 'Everybody has this problem.'

'Well, if everybody has a problem, there has to be a solution,' I told him.

We heard about a guy who had given up his job to set

up a company cabling houses, and we thought, 'bingo!' We chased him down and discovered as much as we could about the emerging market, learning, for example, that 40 per cent of new homes in the United States at the time were being built with some kind of cabling system – and a lot of them had timber frames.

Derek Roddy and I effectively set up Smarthomes while sitting on two bar stools in a hotel in Chicago on that trip.

'What d'you think of the idea?' he asked me.

'Well, I've researched many business ideas for people,' I said. 'I've seen many companies starting up. I know that I personally would put in that system, and if I would, other people would. But where's the plan? Everything happens in Ireland after it happens in America, but the gap – right now – is too big. The building market isn't ready for cabling systems, broadband is only beginning. If we set up a company now, we're too early. Everything's about timing. But if we set it up when the technology's available, we'll be too late. We have to get moving and be ready to go in about three years' time.'

We spent those three years researching. In July 2000, I left the Enterprise Board and got myself a little office. Twelve months later, when we'd proved the concept by piloting it with about forty homeowners, Derek left his job and joined me.

In each of those houses, every single room, when we'd done our job, had a phone and internet connection and opposite the bed there was a TV point – a special TV point, with four connections. One for telephone. One for internet. One for the TV – regular aerial TV. One for satellite TV. All of those were numbered and cabled back to a central hub. It meant that if you wanted to turn the spare bedroom into an office, your main phone line came in through the main hub and you simply had to connect to the right number, which meant that you could set up your complete office with phone, fax and internet, in twenty seconds. It meant that every room had the flexibility to be whatever you wanted it to be at any stage. People had all the services wherever they wanted them, whenever they wanted them, without having to rip up floorboards and bore holes in the walls of a new house.

The only problem was that we were bringing four cables into a house, which made no sense, so I would end up – having gone to Dublin to meet homeowners or builders potentially interested in our product – travelling back home and writing up a presentation at eleven o'clock at night. We would take out a simple machine and join up and measure cables, so that the labour requirement when that cable went on site was simply to pull it from the central location. Nothing else.

Electricians, in common with everybody else, go for the low-hanging fruit. The easiest option. So if three cables would do, they'd put in three cables. By doing everything on a system, we ensured four cables always went in. By colour-coding them, we ensured they couldn't be put in the wrong places. By drawing the house and an elevation of the wall and colour-coding it, we further insured against error. The back box out of which the cables emerged was painted, too.

What we were teaching ourselves was that if you wanted volume and quality in this area, you had to de-skill it. It wasn't about technology now – it was about a process and procedure.

Volume was critical. Doing 50 houses a year was not

enough. We had to build a company capable of volume. In 2002, we did fifty houses. In 2006, we did 2,500 houses. We had built a model that could scale.

In relation to quality, I read all the books and came to the conclusion that most of them are just jargon.

'Quality is an annoying attention to detail,' is our mantra.

Our guys have that annoying attention to detail.

The next priority was to put in an R&D department, because everything is about innovation: it's about seeing the next thing before it happens. Entrepreneurs imagine things before they've happened.

The last thing was the brand. I love brands. When I go to the supermarket, I buy Fairy Liquid. I never think of buying anything else. I buy Daz, because that's what I grew up with. I buy the same stuff because I get a degree of comfort from knowing that the brand means it must be fairly decent stuff, whereas a 'yellow pack' may be cheaper but doesn't give me that reassurance.

I love everything about a brand – its colour, its feel, all the messages it sends about quality. If I see someone driving a flashy BMW, I decide something about the owner.

'Young, sexy man or woman about town,' I think.

If I see someone driving around in a Volvo, or an Audi, I figure the driver is more solid, reliable, not as flighty. If I see someone driving around in a Merc, I think 'Solid, have arrived.' (That's why I've never bought a Merc, because I haven't arrived yet. I drive a Volkswagon Jeep, because it's a workhorse and sends a message the first car I used to drive onto sites – a battered Primera – definitely didn't send.)

The name of our company came from a brainstorming session. I'm a great believer in getting older heads who have some experience and asking for their help, because most entrepreneurs are only too happy to tell their story and share their experience. We brought in two people who subsequently became non-executive directors: Aiden Donnelly was a local guy who'd become MD of Xerox. Gerry McCaughey was MD of Century Homes.

I had initially called the company Home Wiring Systems, but that confused us in people's minds with electricians. When we started looking at names, we settled on the word 'smart', giving us Smarthomes, with the slogan 'Wiring homes for the future'. That sustained us for two years until, at trade shows, people began to make a comment that stuck with me.

'Is it not all gone wireless?' they'd ask.

The reference to wiring was making us redundant, while narrowing us down to one element of the three things we did: cable the house internally, add on the screens or music systems, and finally work with the Eircoms and the NTLs and the Skys to achieve connectivity. We adjusted the brand accordingly:

Smarthomes. Well Connected.

The logo was based on black, because it's impressive, with orange added because it's a dynamic and exciting and bright colour. Because I'm a Cavanman, I have a genetic pre-disposition not to spend money, so I didn't invest much in it until I encountered a builder who was never shy about offering his opinions.

'That Cavan attitude you have will get you nowhere,' he told me. 'Comin' out with cheaper brochures and business cards. That'll get you nowhere. Lemme give you a bit of advice. Go spend money on your brand and on your marketing, because that goes before you and introduces you to people who don't know you.'

I went off immediately and got a professional firm in Donnybrook to come up with colour schemes and designs, and we've used their work right across our materials.

We have a fleet of vans travelling throughout the country-side with our livery, our logo and our website on them. Every-thing now has a colour continuity throughout.

I want the Smarthomes brand to be more than a brand. I want it to serve as a validation, like a crest, like a stamp of approval. I want Smarthomes to stand for a particular stan-dard, giving the kind of reassurance someone gets when they want a sparkling water but they order and get a Ballygowan.

Capitalising the company was interesting.

'Don't go to the bank manager when you need money,' I had always said to people on my start your own business courses. 'Go to the bank manager before you need money.'

So Derek and I walked into the bank manager's office, early on, and planked down our box on his desk.

'I want to tell you about my dream,' I said. 'I want to share with you what we're going to do, and I want you to sit back and relax for ten minutes because I don't want any money from you.'

I had only started about five minutes, when he leaned forward in the chair.

'I have three daughters,' he said. 'Two doing the Leaving,

one in college. I have spent the weekend in the attic trying to get cables down to their rooms, because they have my office in the house tortured trying to get on the internet.'

He called in the assistant manager, who was in the middle of building a house.

'Come in here 'til I tell you about this,' he told her.

'Bingo,' I thought. 'This man is now our ambassador. If he can understand the concept so quickly, we're flying.' At the end of the presentation, he asked me what we might need.

'You're the bank manager here,' I said. 'How much money could you give me without having ask Dublin for approval?'

'€70,000. What would you think you'll need?'

'€65,000,' I shot back at him instinctively. But I don't need it now. When I do, I'll come back to you.'

Every month – just as I had advised participants on start your own business courses – I'd send him a cutting from a newspaper showing a new contract we had secured, or an award we had won, in order to continually build up his confidence in us. But I still didn't go back to him for five years. For the first two years, I took no salary and when Derek joined me after the first year, he became a 50 per cent partner on the basis that he would not take his salary for two years. He could earn his money anywhere he liked, as long as he didn't take it out of the business. I could earn my money wherever I liked on the same basis. I've seen so many people start a new business, get venture capital or borrowing, buy a new car, and be a man about town.

'We're going to do this right,' I said. 'Modestly and organically.'

I moonlighted in the evenings, writing grant forms for local football clubs to get them lottery funding or other funding for their sports halls and facilities. When I was in the Enterprise Board, I became chairman of the national group of business advisors. It was now paying off as many of them brought me around to their counties to give talks on business planning and motivation. That kept me living and paying my mortgage back. Anything either of us had left over, we ploughed back into the business.

Smarthomes as a company was launched in September 2002. In 2004, we turned our first million. In 2006, we went to five million. In 2007, we did eight million. In 2008, we'll go to fifteen. We got to a million euro turnover, eighteen employees and respectable profit levels without ever borrowing a penny or having a bank overdraft. It was only when we got to 2006 that I went for a BES (Business Expansion Scheme). I didn't want venture capital, although venture capitalists play a key role in enterprise development. They share the risk and take a high proportion of the reward. I didn't want a venture capitalist taking 50 per cent of our business at that early stage. I had seen what happened to two entrepreneurs in the UK, of whom I was in awe, until I went over and met them. They got the venture capital in. They bought the flash cars. They got the marketing, but had no organisation to deliver what was promised. The venture capitalists brought in a CEO to get the return they needed and the entrepreneurs ended up with about 7 per cent of their own business.

'I'm going to make a prediction,' I said to Derek when we were on our way back from meeting all the people involved.

'In twelve months' time, we'll be able to buy this company, if we want to, for next to nothing.'

That's what happened. And that was an important lesson for us. There's an arrogance, sometimes, in some entrepreneurs, that prevents them learning from other people's mistakes. I love old people. I really do. They've been through the mill, and you can learn so much from them if you're prepared to say 'What do you think? What would you do?'

The BES scheme gave us the use of €750,000 for five years, paying it back at the end of that period with a markup but without ceding any ownership of the business.

We don't sell features or technology, but that's difficult to get across to someone who's never seen what we do and the difference it could make to them. InterTrade Ireland, at the time, had a competition for the best business plan for the best upcoming company. I wrote our business plan. I tightened it and tightened it again. Then I presented it. We got to the finals and won the national final, 2004 and suddenly found ourselves with €100,000 that we didn't have to repay, not to mention a lot of free public relations. I'm not a lover of advertising, but I am a lover of PR because it's more believable than advertising. The PR was a great launch, and the money allowed us to create a marketing DVD.

'Hold on, now,' I said to myself. 'This is an award-winning business plan. What else can I do in this line?'

The Small Firms Association had their inaugural business awards, and we won the award for most innovative new small company. Then we won the 2005 and 2006 best interior product award from the Construction Industry Federation.

Because growth was beginning to come at this point, we next entered and won the Deloitte rising star award under their 'Fast 50' programme. All I was doing was showing them the business plan and telling them the dream, but supporting it with the facts and figures of our achievements.

In 2006, I got to the finals of the 'Ernst & Young Entrepreneur of the Year'. This gave us media exposure we could never have afforded. It also included a trip to Shanghai, a sort of strategy retreat for CEOs. I wasted no time in expanding my network further to include some of the brightest and best entrepreneurs in the country.

When we started, we worked out of a small room in the Institute of Technology. Just a little incubator space, which was low cost.

'You cannot manage your turnover,' I always said on start your own business courses. 'You can't manage your turnover, because that's outside of your control. But you surely can manage your costs.'

We managed our costs in many ways, not least of them working from this tiny room. Then we moved into a disused bar and gym in Giles' Quay on the Cooley peninsula.

'This is great,' I said. 'It's costing us very little, it has this lovely view of the sea, and I'll be able to walk the beach each lunchtime.' We were there two years. I walked the beach once.

In 2007, we bought a new 30,000 square foot factory in the IDA park in Dundalk. I went back to see the bank manager, who I had assured five years earlier that I would, but this time I wasn't looking for €65,000 but €3m. He said yes.

We're now in the heart of technology businesses, so any-body who comes in sees us as a serious player. We've grown from just Derek and I in 2002 to seventy staff. We're in the north and I'm writing the business plan to take us into the UK in the latter half of 2008.

Whenever, nowadays, entrepreneurs ask me about how we did it, I tell them that, when they identify their dream, they'll write their business plan.

'It will be twice as hard as you ever imagined it was going to be,' I say. 'It will take you twice as long. You will make half as much money. And you will have little time for anything but the business for the first five years. It's the same as if you wanted to be an Olympian athlete. You get up at six in the morning, you train at dawn, you do whatever it takes. You have to have boundless energy. I don't believe that it's possible, in those five years, to have work/life balance. If you're a normal person, you do your job, get out at five, pick up your children, coach the local football team and sit down to read a book at night-time to the backdrop of classical music and your partner gently massaging your feet. It's not like that when you start a business.'

The biggest mistake entrepreneurs make is to allow the company to be over-dependent on them. We have put in a middle management team and structure. We have hired great people and we have put in processes and procedures that will allow the business to operate independent of its owners. It really is about working on the business and not just in the business.

We were the first to market, a sort of 'first mover advantage', which gives a company a certain amount of protection for a limited period of time. We now have competitors we didn't have in the past. Two competitors last year took jobs we should have won, because they went in at such low prices. Both have since gone into liquidation.

Competitors won't have the volume, the quality, the investment in R&D or the brand. Our R&D will allow us to continue to raise the bar by developing more intellectual property, enabling us to move to the next level.

Our R&D has allowed us to move to providing home cinemas, central audio systems and iPod-ready homes. It's taken us to programmable mood lighting systems, electric curtains and blinds and to heating systems controllable from any room. It's taken us to systems allowing busy people to text their homes as they leave their offices, telling it to turn on the immersion heater and the central heating so they can arrive home to a lovely warm house. Our systems can be controlled from anywhere in the world.

The real function of R&D is simple. A few years ago, if you found a kettle in a hotel bedroom for making a cup of coffee, that was something special. Now it's standard. Once you have a product that becomes standard, you have to augment it. You have to produce a better quality product with more services and facilities, and doing it faster and better than anybody else can do it.

My personal focus has changed, too. When you start a business, you have to be a generalist, from cleaning the floor to doing deliveries to collecting the cash and doing work on site. That doesn't work after the first year or two. You have to play to your strengths and get in people who can play to theirs. It's all about getting the right people on the bus.

The 2007 general election in Louth was a fiercely contested one. The biggest challenge for Fianna Fáil was to secure the re-election of its party chairman, Seamus Kirk, a man with twenty-five years' experience as a TD. With a lot left to contribute, he had been written off by the opposition, by most political commentators and even some within Fianna Fáil itself. I was asked, and accepted the challenge, to direct his election campaign. For six months we planned, organised and all but choreographed his campaign, resulting in him not only not losing his seat but actually topping the poll with more than 10,000 first preference votes, an increase of some 54 per cent on the 2002 election result. It summed up politics for me: a good candidate, a strong team and an intelligent electorate. Reflecting on the result, it appears that our business is no different: we have a good product, we have built a strong team to deliver it and we have, increasingly, better-educated and informed customers.

Over the intervening twenty-five years I did complete the last of my five goals. I got a black belt in judo and a black belt in karate and became a qualified fitness instructor, so I understand the importance of fitness, but – over the past few years – I haven't spent enough time on fitness and the physical and mental benefits it brings.

I'm writing a new life plan now. It has a wider degree of awareness than the one I wrote at eighteen. I did all of the things that were in that first plan. I want to be the best person I can be and the most successful, right across the board. In three years' time, when Smarthomes is in the UK and successful in Europe, I would hope to be on to the next thing, the next project. And I want more personal time, for family and friends, and more time for self-improvement which Stephen Covey describes as 'sharpening the saw' in his book, *The Seven Habits of Highly Effective People*.

Periwinkles as Seed Capital

Padraig Ó Ceidigh, Aer Arann

The first seed capital I ever employed was periwinkles. There for the taking. Ready to invest. Bags of periwinkles paid for my first bike, for example. And for my first trip to Dublin, too.

When we were kids growing up in Spiddal, Co. Galway, we used to pick periwinkles on the seashore to help pay for the niceties in life. It was a good life, too. A challenging life, but it was enjoyable, and I suppose that background helped make me the person I am.

I should have been a plumber. That was my plan. I sometimes think when I see the money those guys make that not being a plumber was my first big mistake. My parents must have wondered what would happen when I went to university – would they have a teacher or a lawyer or an accountant in the family? As it turned out they got all three. I tried all of them before I got involved with Aer Arann. In fact, it was walking along a beach that led me to Aer Arann. There I was, wandering a beach in the west, when I came upon a spot where digging was going on.

'Now what's that about?' I wondered. 'Hey, you know what this is. This is an airstrip. Now, whoever is building this is either crazy or they're about to do something fantastic.'

I'd no idea what the purpose of the airstrip was, but I just liked the idea of it in the middle of nowhere. So I set about finding out who was building it. It turned out to be a guy named Tom Kilroe, who was in his fifties at that time. Born in Roscommon, like a lot of people of his generation he went to Manchester without a penny in his pocket and just did labouring, working his way up to owning a hotel, among other things. He was setting up this airstrip to fly planes over to the Aran Islands and back. He had a concession from the Irish government to fly two nine-seater planes.

A guy once said that you can only join the dots of life by looking back. It's only in hindsight, by reflecting on the past, that you can say 'Oh my good God, this happened because of this, that, or the other.' It's a mistake to believe you can plan your life. The reality is that you can never really know what's around the corner.

I got more and more fascinated by this tiny airline, and eventually I made an offer to buy it. Tom was happy enough to sell because he could see my enthusiasm, and he figured I'd take it much further than he could.

Then another happy accident happened. Happy for me, anyway. A small airline that had a contract to run flights to an airfield in Donegal went bust. I tendered to replace them.

On the face of it, it made no sense. Only nine months of the contract remained. But I wanted to expand. I really wanted to expand. Then I got a call from a contact in the Department of Communications.

'I've got good news and bad news for you,' he began. 'Which would you like first?'

'Gimme the good news first, 'cause when I have that, the bad news'll be easier to take on board.'

'The good news is that you've won the contract.'

'Well, that's great,' I said. 'I don't care what the bad news is, it couldn't be that bad, given that I've won the contract. That's fantastic.'

'The bad news is that the first flight has to happen on Monday.' This was Friday. I had no plane.

'Let's be very clear,' the department official told me. 'You can have this contract only if you start running planes on Monday. Simple as that.'

I rang Tom Kilroe and leased a plane from him for £1,800 a day. That plane flew the route on Monday. I was in business. I was expanding. I did, however, have one small problem, which was that the cost of leasing the plane was more than the value of the contract. I had to get a plane of my own. Now, around this time, I was spending a lot of time at Dublin airport and I'd noticed a Shorts 360 sitting idle there. I got on the blower to find out who owned it. It turned out to be a UK private company with a business mainly in freight transport but doing some passenger flights, too.

'Will you let me have this plane, since you don't seem to be using it much?' I asked them.

'OK, but we've a contract requiring the plane to go to the Isle of Man and back once a day carrying passengers,' they said.

'Who the hell goes to the Isle of Man that often?'

'Mostly bankers.'

'Oh. Fine. Let me take the plane and I'll take responsibility for flying the bankers to the Isle of Man and back every day too.'

That little plane started lashing back and forth between Donegal and the Isle of Man every day. Just about breaking even. Just about.

It was great. Every day was different for me. I was going hard, working for twelve, fourteen or maybe sixteen hours a day. I didn't have an office. Still don't. Never had an office in my life. My office is my mobile phone, the car and the aeroplane and I meet people on the go and I need to be where it's at and where things are happening so I don't wait for life or business to come to me. I go out and I engage in life and engage in business.

Which is how I had a chance encounter at Croke Park. I was queuing for a sandwich at half time when I got chatting to a fellow beside me. It turned out he was in the freight business and had to deliver goods every day from Ireland to Coventry. And back. By the time the sandwich was finished, my Shorts 360 had more work to do. Now, it was on the go from eight in the morning until two the following morning. First, it took the bankers to the Isle of Man, then did the Donegal trip, then went back to the Isle of Man to pick up the bankers.

When it came back, me and the lads would be waiting with a Hi-ace van. We'd strip the seats out of it, put them in the van, and send the plane flying off to Coventry with a freight load. It would arrive back at two in the morning, and

we'd put the seats back in, ready for the dawn flight to the
Isle of Man.

The difficult thing – the exciting thing – was that we had so
little room for manoeuvre. If anything went off-schedule, any
time during the day, we had a real problem. It was incredibly
stressful. After a bit of persistent door-knocking, I got to see
Larry Stanley, CEO of Aer Lingus at the time. I got straight
to the point with him.

'Larry, I want to build a regional airline,' I told him. 'I don't
think Aer Lingus needs to be running the regional flights
within Ireland. So why don't you let Aer Arann do them?'

He was initially intrigued with the idea, but after some
discussions the idea petered out. Aer Lingus couldn't see much
in it for them. I did, however, develop a relationship with Larry
Stanley, so he became a director of Aer Arann after he left Aer
Lingus.

GALWAY COUNTY LIBRARIES

At this time, I was driving from Spiddal to Dublin and
back six days a week. I did that for seven years. A typical
day might involve leaving the house at five and getting back
between eight and midnight. Even on Sundays, there was the
odd interruption. I remember a woman calling to the door of
the house unannounced, just as we were beginning a Sunday
lunch.

'I've driven forty miles to see you,' was her opening gambit.
'I want to talk to you about a job for my son …'

The curious thing is that, once you're in the airline business, everybody assumes you know everything about air travel
and that you can solve all problems. I get weird phone calls.

'I hate to trouble you,' one of them began, 'but my husband

is in Dublin and has to catch a flight this morning to New York
but he left his passport behind here in Galway. It's desperately
important that the passport gets to Dublin. Would there be
any chance you could put it on the morning plane?'

The only way to handle this kind of call is to be scrupu-
lously polite, as helpful as possible – and get the phone
number changed again and again and keep it secret for as long
as possible ...

My background is working class from rural Ireland. I went
to a Jesuit secondary school in Galway where one of the big
challenges for me was that people there were, obviously, speaking English while I came from an Irish-speaking background.

Even now I actually think in Irish and speak in English.
I see that not as a disadvantage, but rather as a big advantage
to me now. But back then, it complicated my life. I was not
really focused on going to college. I went to that school simply
because my best friend went there. I knew nothing about the
school. Insofar as I had an ambition, it was for plumbing.

But my teachers and the principal strongly encouraged me.
They also met my parents and said, 'This guy should go to
college.'

I did reasonably well in the Leaving Cert which meant I
could have done a number of different courses and degrees
in college. The only reason I did a commerce degree was because my best teacher, the teacher I admired most in secondary school, was our commerce teacher. I chose a school and a
discipline based on friendship and admiration of other people,
rather than on any kind of formal career guidance. That's just
the way the dots fell. The dots could have fallen in a quite

different way. If, for example, the best teacher was a science teacher or the best teacher was a geography teacher I would have pursued a different career in college. The degree I ended up doing is another dot in my life's pattern that got joined by accident.

In college I befriended guys who were involved in Irish, in the Irish language and who played hurling and football. I hung around with guys like Joe Connolly who was captain of the Galway hurling team that won the All-Ireland in 1980. He was the man who made that famous 'people of Galway we love you' speech.

Those guys helped me develop the passion I have for where I am and where I came from and who I am. That passion is pivotal to my life, and I have made very sure I never lost it. You can't afford to lose your roots or your respect for where you came from, whether that's from a financially well-to-do family or the opposite end of the street where we came from. Your roots, your sense of belonging are equally important in who you become, no matter what part of Ireland you were born in. I think it is important to be proud of who you are, what made you. So it's probably no coincidence that I still live in Spiddal with Caitlín and our four children.

My parents had a really great influence on me. All parents do, I believe.

Like a lot of people today I can see that my parents' lives were unbelievably different from mine. I drive a Lexus. Neither of them would ever have earned the money to own a Lexus. Both came from a working-class background, which constrained their choices. Because there was no work in Connemara when they were growing up, they had to emigrate. They went to England – to London – and they met in a famous place where Irish people were meeting at that time – a ballroom called the Galtymore in Cricklewood.

They met at an Irish dance, developed a relationship and got married in London – and I was the oldest of five kids. At that stage, they decided to move back to Ireland. If they hadn't made that decision, my life would have been unimaginably different, and I might be living in London right here and now. I could have an English accent and be the guy wearing a Glasgow Celtic jersey or a Manchester United jersey. Who knows what would have happened if my life had taken that direction?

But instead they came back home, bringing the whole family of youngsters with them in a pretty fundamental move for my parents which inevitably had a big bearing on the lives of all of their children.

We moved back to Spiddal. My father was not the oldest son and at that time the eldest son would be given the farm. Not that the farm was big. Our farm was maybe twelve acres of land at best with probably two thirds of it full of rocks. That's why we spent so much of our time along the shore picking periwinkles, which is not a bad existence at all.

After I did the commerce degree, I went on to train as a chartered accountant with KPMG, but I knew fairly quickly that it wasn't the right job for me. So I qualified in law. Then I had a go at teaching. In fact, I spent eleven years teaching maths at Coláiste Iognáid, a Jesuit boys' school in Galway. In the early 1990s I decided to take a career break and try my hand as a solicitor, but while I liked the court work, as with accountancy I found being at a desk quite boring.

The fact that I stopped teaching doesn't mean I didn't love it. I did love teaching. Above all the things I've done in my life, teaching is the one I enjoyed most. I used to get my kids to write their own Leaving Certificate maths books because the people who write maths books – how do they know how my kids, my students, learn, how they pick up information? Each student is different. Each class is different. Each Leaving Cert year is quite different. As a teacher, you need to be really close to them in order for them to absorb and really understand what you are trying to pass on.

I never came across a bad student in my life. I came across bad teachers who were uninterested, unfocused, undisciplined, with no drive, no initiative. Now I'm not saying all teachers are bad teachers, not by a long shot, but I came across teachers who really didn't have the initiative and drive I believe the students deserved. I came across some absolutely wonderful teachers. We all do. We all come across some wonderful teachers that we still look back on in awe, because they inspire you to do things that you felt you couldn't do.

I'm not saying that I made the best decision leaving teaching, but having said that, despite being close to my pupils and enjoying it hugely, teaching was like being in a straitjacket. I couldn't do things I wanted to do. I was already a qualified solicitor when I was teaching and I wanted to teach law to the kids. I met the Secretary of the Department of Education and I said I'd like to teach law – I had a book written at the time on basic law for school kids.

'Why do you want to teach law, for God's sake?' he asked me. 'We've got a wide curriculum already.'

'They've been teaching law to sixteen-year-olds in England for the past fifty years,' was my response. 'Surely kids should know their rights when they get summer jobs or when they are buying clothes or whatever. Just let me teach law as a pilot scheme in the Jesuit school in Galway.'

It didn't happen. It just didn't happen. This was an initiative that had no downside to it, but when you're proposing anything related to the public or the civil service in this country, you quickly find that there is a process which governs the entire thing, and you have no choice but to get sucked into that process. Then you have to wait years and years and years to change the process from within.

I'm not the kind of guy who is willing to wait and I just don't hang around. I'll actually change things if I can but I couldn't change the Department of Education because there are processes and procedures – and I'm sure for very, very good reasons – but those processes and procedures, no matter how valid they may be, tend to make guys and girls who think like me extremely frustrated.

I believe that's one of the hidden reasons for what's called 'natural wastage' within the teaching profession. The teachers with ideas, the teachers with initiative, the teachers who would like to change and improve things end up leaving the job, and in some cases – I'm not saying in my case – that's a pity because they have a big contribution to make.

Our education system is the heart of the Celtic Tiger and I really appreciate and respect that. But its big weakness is that we teach people *what* to learn, we don't teach them *how* to learn. There's a big difference. When I was teaching, I tried to teach kids how to learn. In other words, if you know how your mind works, if you know how best you absorb information, whether through visual or auditory or other means, you can learn learning techniques, rather than simply ingesting data.

Precisely the same capacities which made me leave teaching were the traits an entrepreneur needs. It comes back to passion. Entrepreneurs have to have a passion, a willingness to jump outside their comfort zone and hope it is not into deep water or quicksand. You really don't know what you're going to land in. All you can hope for is that you will hit solid ground. Real entrepreneurs all share that willingness to go outside their comfort zone. To non-entrepreneurs it often looks reckless. It can look like madness.

When I bought Aer Arann, for example, most people would have regarded it as madness. Particularly for an ex-teacher who was also an ex-solicitor. But I had a gut feeling and so I re-mortgaged the house. In 1994 the company owned two planes and had a turnover of €250,000. Today, we have fourteen planes, we carry 1.2 million passengers a year. We have a turnover of €100 million.

I did dive into really deep water when I took it over and I had to learn to swim fast in an area where I had no experience. That meant learning an awful lot very quickly. When you're running a new business while learning at the same time, you just go like the hammers of hell. When the waters become a little bit calmer, the temptation is to believe that you have the whole thing under control, but that's not true. The waters get turbulent again for all sorts of reasons that are outside of your control. Then they get calm again. That's life – I'm still not ashore.

I suppose I got into it because I believe in living life, doing what you can and doing your best. Sometimes doing your best will work and sometimes it won't work. You're going to have people out there in the pub and in the media saying 'Who the hell does he think he is?' Unfortunately, there's a lot of negativity out there.

But what matters is when you can go home at night to your husband or wife and family and you can sit down and look into the fire.

'Dammit, I did my best,' I say to myself in that situation. 'I did my best and I don't give a damn what other people think because I didn't do it for ego, I didn't do it for power and control, I did it because I had a conviction and I wanted to make a change and I did my best – that's all anybody can do.'

I've a big problem about people who live lives just to be like the Joneses or to have cars like other people or to do things just the way other people do. It's important to do your best but it is also important not to be afraid to move on.

Entrepreneurs are highly influenced by outside forces. But we develop a gut feeling, a sixth sense which helps us distil the important stuff. I don't separate my personal life from my professional persona. I don't put on a suit and become Padraig Ó Ceidigh, the entrepreneur, and then take it off and become somebody else.

I get sixty or seventy emails a day, as a lot of people do. I get maybe twenty to forty phone calls a day. I don't know for sure.

I never counted them but I get a serious number. Plus I have anything from four to twelve meetings a day, every day. So there's a lot of information overload there. But entrepreneurs have to learn very quickly to distinguish between information and knowledge because a maximum 1 per cent of all information that comes your way is knowledge you need in order to make decisions. The other 99 per cent is fluff.

We all make the wrong decision sometimes. And yes, sometimes I feel like giving up. I think it's bullshit when people say, 'I was never going to give up, I knew I'd always get there.' We're all human – and everybody at times feels like giving up and saying this won't work, I'm going to throw in the towel. You keep going and you keep trying and you keep doing your best.

Just as persistence is a vital trait in an entrepreneur, so is having the wit to realise when persistence is pointless and knowing when to give up. John Wayne famously once said: 'Hey, young man, when you're on a dead horse, the best thing to do is get off it.' If things aren't working out you've got to realise that and move on to the next gig. Sometimes people stay on for too long.

What I hate doing is letting other people down. We all let people down. You cannot go through life without at some stage letting people down. I did it recently to really good hard-working staff. We outsourced our ground-handling in Dublin and that affected fifty-four staff members. Those staff members were people who had been taken on in the previous two and a half years. Really good people who worked hard for the company. We had to do it, though, in order to cut costs.

We did make sure that every single one of those people had a job when we agreed the outsourcing contract. We guaranteed them a job but it wasn't with Aer Arann and a number of them were deeply disappointed. I know they feel I let them down and that bothers me. It does bother me. But we had to do it for the sake of the company overall.

I do see myself moving on from Aer Arann at some point. Aer Arann is not life. Aer Arann is part of life. It's a transition process. I don't see Aer Arann as something that I'll hold on to, close to my heart and close to my pocket. I don't have the dynastic thing which would anticipate that my kids will come up and start running the company. No. They're going to do their things. They're going to walk in a field full of corn that's three foot high on sunny days and on rainy days and they'll create their own path and they will not follow in the path that their dad created. At least I hope they won't. They will start doing their own thing. I know they would not do what I'm doing because of the effort it takes and the stress you put yourself under and I wouldn't disagree with them there.

My kids think I work really hard. They think I work too hard. They think I make myself available to people too much; they think that I haven't given them enough time, which is true at different times. I know they feel proud of me – I know that. It's not easy for me to say but I know they do. And they support me a lot, big time.

Aer Arann takes an enormous amount of my time, but it does it productively. When I was teaching in a secondary school, I suppose I was working 174 days out of 365 days a year. Each day, I would have been working for about four or

five hours a day. Multiply the number of days by the number
of hours worked and you'll end up with a total that's perhaps
less than one thousand hours a year. I do a thousand hours in
a handful of weeks now.

But I do things to relax too. I run marathons. I run half
marathons. I go out twice, three times a week – I'd run four
to six to seven miles. In October 2006, I did Route 66. I went
across America on a Harley Davidson with sixty-five mad
Irish people and that was relaxation. You're there rolling down
the road, like an Eagles song, the wind blowing in your face
and, although there were other guys around, you existed in
your own space. I did that for ten days. What a retreat …

I also relax by being at home with my family, doing nothing or watching TV. I relax by going to football games with
my son. I relax by learning. I love learning. I relax by meeting
people. I enjoy meeting new people and different people and
different backgrounds and learn about them and they learn
about me.

I can switch off. Business doesn't have to be 24/7. It may
have to be that demanding in the early days of an enterprise,
but it should not continue at that level. I've learned to discipline my mind in order to switch off.

There are things that once upon a time would have hurt
me personally, things I would have carried around so that
I would be eaten up inside by them, but I've learned how
to control that as well, partly because I've started reading
about emotions. One of the books that greatly influenced me
is *Emotional Intelligence* by a guy named Daniel Goldman.
I found that helpful. I found out that by controlling your

emotions you can control your life and you can control your attitude to life. You can choose how to react to things that life throws at you.

If something upsets you, you have to learn to step back, maybe go for a walk by the sea or for a pint in Hughes' pub. You cool yourself down and then it's not such a big issue.

That's self control and self discipline.

There's good and bad in everything and I try to deal with the bad in a positive way. We all meet grief, sadness, death, sickness and injury. People may knife you in the back and attack you for no apparent reason. It happens to all of us, unfortunately. I believe it is part of the whole testing in life that we go through.

I got good advice once from a wise man whose son had been killed in a car crash. Somebody was giving me a hard time and I told him about it: 'You know, Padraig,' he said to me. 'If I were you I'd say a prayer for that lady because life must be very tough for her.' Since then, I have tried to understand that when people are in despair or really eaten up inside they can lash out expressing anger, venom even.

The people I really admire are those who have suffered unimaginable pain but who can still forgive. People who maybe lost a kid or a brother or sister or a parent, for example in Northern Ireland.

You know what they do? They pray for the person who actually killed their child or their mother. That's the most powerful thing on earth. If the rest of us could do that with just the small knives that are thrown in our direction, life would be much different.

It is true that life is a journey, not a destination, and we have to enjoy the journey.

There's a really great book called *The Four Agreements*, based on the Toltec civilisation who were in Mexico hundreds of years ago. Their philosophy was to take nothing personally, even when you are attacked for no good reason. You create a space around yourself to protect you from the venom and you understand that the person is doing it because they are suffering. We can't choose what happens to us but we do choose how to react, and if you react in a positive way life will be better.

Failure is part of life too and we all fail in different ways at different times in our lives. In the United States 92 per cent of all new businesses fail after five years. Imagine: only 8 per cent are successful. It's the same kind of ratio for salmon going up river to spawn but the salmon keep going.

I would just tell people to go for it. Maybe we all come back here and live life a second time, third time, fourth time, or fifth time. I really don't know but I know we're here now and I would say take the chance, go up in the balloon, see where it brings you. Maybe you won't learn to fly it or you may not land where you expected to but you will have an adventure. I think life is an adventure. It's all an adventure.

The most important asset any of us has is not money but intelligence. A long time ago I decided that my best resource was what was between my ears and I decided to learn about learning. I started learning about how the mind works, how the brain works, how memory works. I used that when I was teaching. I developed strategies that would be called 'accelerated learning' now. That's why I got my students to write their own maths books.

I worked as an accountant, a solicitor, a teacher and at marketing but the skillsets that helped me most in business were those I picked up as a teacher.

It's all about people and dealing with people and adults are only grown up kids at the end of the day. One of my passions is to mentor or support other people who want to set up a business. I recently met a guy at the end of a fairly tough day who asked could he bounce a few ideas off me. We chatted until past midnight. I gave him my views and my thoughts, for what they're worth. Hopefully he'll set up a business, create employment and help make this great country a better country, and that means a lot to me.

One thing I really believe in is continuous learning. I use every opportunity to learn, I take at least a week out every year and I do what I call a business retreat. I have gone to the United States, I have gone to the UK and to other countries. I'm just back from a three-week stint at Harvard University. I was invited to give a talk to students there and I took the opportunity to study for three weeks with about 100 business people. I found that exhilarating.

You learn from different cultures, how they look at business, how they develop business, how they develop entrepreneurial skills and so on. I've been very involved with the Entrepreneur of the Year programme and I've learned a lot from that too. Ireland is a small place with a population of four million or thereabouts. There's 300 million in America. There are 70 million people in Egypt and we don't consider Egypt a significant country. I believe there are huge opportunities in places like Egypt. You could pick any place.

The Australians are great people, hugely entrepreneurial. They live on a huge big island that's thousands of miles from places like the United States.

Those guys know two things. They know how to do business and they know how to party.

I don't believe in putting on a show to suit the occasion. The reactions inside are the reactions you'll see. I don't really think about when I need to smile or whether I should be cross in a certain situation. Whatever is inside comes out. Life is easier that way.

It's not like the poem, *The Love Song of J. Alfred Prufrock*, where the guy has to react differently in public depending on the different people he meets or the different situations he finds himself in.

I always look forward to tomorrow, regardless of the challenge ahead. There have of course been times when I've stayed up at night worrying.

I remember once I was addressing a major forum organised by the Western Development Commission in Kiltimagh which was attended by about 500 people. Miriam O'Callaghan of RTÉ was the chairperson and I was in the middle of my great talk about my vision for air services in the west of Ireland when Miriam tapped on the microphone and cut me dead.

'Padraig, I'm just curious,' she said. 'I want to ask you a question. I can't help it, I know I'm breaking your flow.'

Five hundred people were wondering what was coming next and I was wondering myself.

'Padraig, a straight question. How do you sleep at night?'

'Miriam, I sleep like a baby,' I responded. 'I wake up every hour crying.'

And that is true. Sometimes. Because I'm only human. There are pressures and stresses on us all and you do wake up worried about things. Thank God it's not as frequently as it used to be, and when you've good people around you, a great wife and great kids, you can go into your cave, into your home and it kind of protects you and shields you against a lot of the outside world. But I never wake up in the morning and say, 'I wish I wasn't here.'

I wake up in the morning and say, 'It's a new day, I'm going to give it my best shot.'

That's how I'd like to be remembered. When the time comes I'd like them to say, 'He did his best.'

I don't worry about that day coming. I'm just going to enjoy the journey. And join up the dots later.

It Started on *The Late Late Show*

John Concannon,
JFC Manufacturing Co. Ltd

It started on *The Late Late Show*. Literally. My entire business. I was thirty-one years old, married with four kids, and I had invented a joined-up set of plastic buckets, because feeding calves with one bucket drove me mad.

You could never hold the bucket because one calf would have his head in it and he'd push it and spill it and the other calves would be pushing to get at it. I'd be trying to hold a few buckets together with my fingers and one day I just stuck two buckets together, held by a bit of wood. Then I put three together, with a link to keep them steady. It was a common sense thing to do. Not just for me – for every farmer trying to feed calves.

Once I had a product I decided I needed publicity. Back in 1986/87, *The Late Late Show* was the place to be. It was top of the pops in the TV ratings. So I went straight into RTÉ and put my bucket thing up on the reception desk.

'I want to talk to Gay Byrne,' I told the receptionist, who gently explained that it doesn't work like that.

'But Brigid Ruane is his researcher,' she said, helpfully.

'All right, I'll talk to Brigid Ruane.'

'You can't get to see her, either.'

'Well, I'm leaving these buckets for her.'

Any time I was in Dublin after that I would leave one of the bucket sets in RTÉ with Brigid Ruane's name on it. She must have ended up with five or six, but I was still getting nowhere. I got a guy to write a professional letter to her about the virtues of my joined-up buckets. That met with silence, too. Then, amazingly, one Friday morning I got a call out of the blue.

'You're on tomorrow night,' I was told.

They must have had a cancellation or something, but I didn't care. I didn't even have a suit. A friend of mine had a man's shop and he helped me pick a suit after hours on the Friday night. It was a big thing getting on *The Late Late Show*. But the real motivation was that my friend, Martin McHale, had bet me a hundred quid that I'd never get on *The Late Late Show*.

'Give me until the end of the year,' I told him when we made the bet in springtime. It was 18 December 1987 when I got the call, so I won the bet.

I was supposed to get two minutes on RTÉ, but it stretched out, so I actually got twelve minutes on prime time TV. Mega stuff. Gay Byrne went to town on it. The audience laughed, they thought it was so funny. Rolf Harris was on the same night, and the marvellous thing was that he referred to it a good few times during the show when he was being interviewed, in spite of me insulting him in the hospitality room before we went on. (I thought he was Roger Whittaker and

told him I was a big fan – of Roger Whittaker. Talk about getting it wrong in one easy lesson …)

On the night, I was photographed with Gay Byrne and the
bucket, so when we had our first newsletter, our first brochure,
we had Gay Byrne in it. We got tremendous mileage out of
that. The newspapers would take any story with his face on it.

Gay Byrne was so fantastic to us. I met him recently in the
Canaries when he was coming back from holidays. I went over
and said who I was and he wanted to know everything about
how the company had progressed. He had a genuine interest
in what I was doing and how the company had grown. He was
a huge contributor to what followed. That one appearance on
The Late Late Show was the foundation of the company – it
went from strength to strength from then on.

Well, maybe 'strength to strength' is a bit of an exagger-
ation, because production wasn't big enough or highly geared
enough at the time to sell the volumes that we could have sold
as a result of that show. Nevertheless, the name was made, the
company was made and I was known far and wide after that.
John Concannon, JFC Manufacturing, Tuam. The man with
the joined-up buckets.

Everyone called me 'the bucket man'.

Brigid Ruane, Gay Byrne and *The Late Late Show* audience all 'got' the joined-up bucket idea. That made a hell of a
change. Before that, when I'd gone to the IDA, they thought
I was off the head. So did Údarás. I failed so miserably trying
to get support for this idea, I realised I needed to be a better
salesman. Brendan Regan in Galway was the guy I talked to.
He had a course coming up. But the cost was £700.

'I don't have £700,' I told him. 'But if I can sell seven of these courses, will I get my own free?'

I think I sold five. In the process, I met up with a guy and managed to sell him a management course and a sales training course. When I was doing the sales pitch to him I told him about my own product idea. He was in the plastic business.

'You know, I might be able to make that,' he said when I was finished.

I went back home, got a prototype and came back to him the next day with it.

'Yes,' he said. 'I think we can make it.'

The next thing I wanted was to get it into the Spring Show awards. The RDS Spring Show was the place to be at the time and I was on a high, figuring I knew how to sell these things. So I entered it in the competition. I convinced the seven or eight judges that this was the greatest thing since the wheelbarrow – and it won. I remember one farmer congratulating me and saying, 'You know something, you must be the laziest man in Ireland. Jaysus. Sticking three buckets together.'

That was his summary of what I did. But it still made sense to him. It made sense to any farmer with calves, because with two sets of Buckatinis, you could feed six calves simultaneously. It was that simple. It solved a farmer's problem. And I knew all about farmers' problems, having grown up on a small farm my father owned.

When I was young I went to all the fairs in the west of Ireland like Ballindine, Kilmane, Ballinrobe, Headford, Tuam, Dunmore, Claremorris. You got to the fair at four or five in the morning with cattle or sheep, put them up against the wall, sold them, slapping hands, counting out cash, wheelin' and dealin'. Dealing. It was all about the deal. It was a farming background, but it was a trading background, too. My father was a good dealer. I watched him at it for years. I learned more from that than I did from school. I was one that didn't go to school when I should have gone to school. I left secondary school after two years and worked with my father. It was very easy to educate me; it was done in two years …

My practical education mostly consisted of learning from mistakes. For example, I used to make money by selling hay. In those days the bales were small and easy to manage. We had good ground for growing hay and it was no bother to cut the hay, make it into bales and load it into a truck. I would drive from farm to farm around Connemara or in the other direction into Limerick or Tipperary to sell the bales. When the weather was wet, which was often, regular customers would be routinely suspicious that the bales might be wet and might rot. I would give them assurances, but the bales would be carefully inspected anyway. The trouble was that the bales might be wet on the outside from being carried in an open truck, and there might be a shower of rain which would make them look wet even though they were dry inside.

One wet day, around Cashel, my biggest customer was cagey about the bales and decided he wasn't buying any this time. He suggested to try The Yank. The Yank was a farmer nearby who had been to America a long time ago and came back with a touch of an accent. It was pouring as I pulled into his yard. He was in a cheerful mood and we had a chat. I got around to asking him if he needed any bales. He said he didn't need any bales, but could do with some ducks.

'Ducks?'

'Yes. Ducks,' he assured me. 'What I need is ducks.'

'Fair enough,' I said and set off again to try to find buyers for my hay.

A woman at home, Mrs Wheelan, had a lot of ducks and it occurred to me that there might be an opportunity here. I talked to her and she agreed to sell me fourteen of them. I took them in the truck on my next outing along with the bales. This was a bit difficult. I had to stack the bales leaving a space for the ducks reinforced by a crossways plank of timber. I eventually arrived at the Yank's farm.

'I have some ducks for you,' I announced.

He looked dumbfounded. Then collapsed laughing. With difficulty, because he couldn't stop laughing, he told me that his reference to ducks was only a joke; a reference to the wet weather.

'No use for ducks,' he told me, still chortling.

I set off with my bales and ducks to see could I retrieve the situation somewhere else. Starting with Tom Burke, a local man who had some ducks.

'Are they ducks or drakes?' he asked.

I hadn't a clue. I had an idea that ducks had a different colour to drakes. But Tom told me that these were young and at that stage you couldn't tell the difference. This was important. Tom would buy ducks but not drakes. He took me and the fourteen ducks into a shed where he had a remarkable routine to, as they say, sort the ducks from the drakes. He put himself in the middle of the ducks so they were circling him randomly. Then, with a small light stick, he would hit one lightly on the tail. If it was a duck it would quack and if it was a drake it wouldn't. It turned out that there were four drakes so I managed to sell the ten ducks.

Years later I was giving a talk at a local conference and I told the duck story, and maybe embellished it a bit, so it got a great reception. I didn't think much more about that until a few months afterwards I volunteered to deliver a load of goods from my factory to Dublin. Even though I'm now the boss of my own company I like to occasionally make a delivery myself, and get talking to other truck drivers – who wouldn't know me – and hear what gossip they have. I parked and went to have a chat with another driver who was lighting up a cigarette. He gave me a funny look as I said something to start up a conversation with him.

'How's the duck business in Connemara then?' he asked.

I could only laugh. That's the great thing about the mistakes you make when you're young: they become funny stories later on, linking you with total strangers. At the time, though, they're not so diverting. Not to me, anyway. I was on the farm, and I was driving a truck. I knew how to deal. I knew how to survive, but I was married and had children and wanted to do more. However, the times weren't great: the interest rate was 18 per cent and jobs were not easy to come by. My big ambition at the time was to earn a £100 a week.

I did a lot of truck-driving, but the first non-farming initiative I took was when I filled the boot of the car up with smoke alarms I'd bought from a company bringing them into

Ireland for the first time. I spent two weeks on the roadside trying to sell those things. It didn't happen. After two weeks on the road, I had sold only one. I abandoned that and went back to the drawing board.

But all the time, in the back of my head, was the calf-feeding idea. Originally, when I got them manufactured, I went to Kerry and started selling them door to door.

I often sold forty in a day. But that was a slow slog. A new word had entered my vocabulary: cashflow. Door-to-door selling meant I had cash to flow for me and the crowd that was supplying to me. I believed then – and I believe now – that you can build a good business by honouring your terms. If you say, 'You're going to get a cheque from me on x date,' you'd better have that cheque there on that date.

The company was formed in 1987 with a £1000 overdraft. The next year I got £1,800 from the Galway County Development Team, which is now the County Enterprise Board, and the manager at the time was Charles Lynch.

Once we had the RDS award and *The Late Late Show*, we were in business. The problem was, we were in too much business. We couldn't deliver on the demand. Our production wasn't geared for the volumes the *Late Late* generated. We should have had them in stock before I went on that programme. I didn't know then that this is a classic mistake of small new companies. They do a big publicity stunt and then can't back it up with deliveries.

On the other hand, our money management was good. Things got better slowly. So the first year, we turned over £18,000. Year two was £55,000. Year three, £120,000. So from the first three years it paid. It didn't even enter my head that it might not succeed, I wanted it to so badly. I really wanted to make this happen. I had to make it happen. I'd been a farmer. I'd been a truck driver, so, used to getting up early, I didn't need an alarm clock. My wife Patricia had basically raised four children on her own. This venture had to succeed.

We got into manufacturing by accident. I was sitting down at dinner with three fellows and one of them mentioned a plastic moulding machine for sale in a company in Donegal that had closed.

'I'd love to see that,' I said. 'I'd have an interest in it.'

'It's sitting in an Údarás na Gaeilge factory that's closed down,' he told me.

The next morning I was in Donegal, in Údarás, looking to talk to the man in charge, whose name, believe it or not, was Daniel O'Donnell.

'Could I speak to Daniel O'Donnell?'

'There's no Daniel O'Donnell here.'

'There has to be.'

'Daniel O'Donnell? No. Oh, you mean Danny! Danny is here, all right.'

Danny was in, so he showed me this factory with one brand new, unused machine in it. Plus an old machine which had come from Crolly dolls. The Crolly doll was once a household name: a little doll from the village of Crolly in Donegal with plastic arms, body, head and legs, dressed up in lovely frilly national costumes – it could be Scottish outfits – put together and dressed up by people in that village. It was a big industry in Donegal at one time. Crolly dolls had also featured on *The Late Late Show* years before our buckets.

The company had gone out of business and this stuff was sitting there. I bought the whole lot. I still have all the tooling and moulds for the Crolly dolls, although we never made them. The other machines were what I was after, even though I didn't even have a factory at the time. Eventually I convinced the IDA to give me a small unit where we located the machines, converted them to our purposes and got them to work. When I bought them, I had no clue about them. But I'm a quick learner. I'm great at trial and error. That was the start of our manufacturing.

After that, reading a newspaper, I spotted a bigger machine for sale in Scotland by a company called McAlpine's. I went to see the machine, realised it was what we needed and indicated interest.

'Write us a letter of offer,' was the response.

Fine. Except I didn't know how to write a letter of offer. So I went to Easons and bought this book, *How to Write a Business Letter*. Lo and behold – wasn't there a sample letter of offer in it for a sewing machine. I just put 'rotation machine' in place of 'sewing machine', offered them £4000 and said 'the offer finishes on the fifteenth of next month.'

We bought it and rebuilt it. Ran it for five or six years and sold it for four times what we gave for it. Off it went to France after we were done with it and we put in a brand new machine in its place. Once we could afford it, I always went for state-of-the-art machinery in every area of our business. That's the only way you can compete, these days, no matter what you produce.

The next product, after the buckets, was a plastic water trough to provide animals with water during the summer season when they were out in the fields. The big seller at the time was the concrete trough, but unfortunately concrete troughs break, because frost will force them to expand and crack. Frost wouldn't have that effect on plastic, so we designed a trough similar to the concrete one, made it in plastic and created a market for it.

Over time, we put a family of products for agriculture together, partly in response to the needs of co-ops. Co-ops don't want a company of one. They don't want a one-product company. They want a range of products.

I learned how to design and develop plastic products and discovered I have a good brain for design. I pulled good sheet metal fabricators around me so we were able to make our own tooling. That was the strength of the company at the start and still is today.

We now have ten or twelve people full time in R&D. For a small company, that's a big research programme. Our products for the agricultural sector are seasonal: once one thing is finished for that year, you need to have something else if you want to have turnover twelve months of the year. However, we expanded beyond that market to develop a portfolio of products we could sell to other sectors. At the moment we do linen trolleys for hotels and for catering and we make bottle banks for Repac.

Some ideas come to fruition quickly, while others might take five years to develop. That's why investment in R&D is important. It fuels growth in the company, delivering the products that come out of it. Products – not 'inventions'. I don't like that word. Inventors are fellas with forty-one ideas who never make a shilling out of any of them. I'd rather take one at a time, develop it, turn it into cash if possible and learn from it if it fails. JFC today make quality products.

One product that failed was a little butter dish. At the time, these light 'butter' spreads were coming on the market, so we developed a little butter dish to accommodate the quarter pound container on the market. The university in Galway did a marketing projection and gave me a report on exactly how good this product would be. In fact, that was the one product that nearly took the company down. We spent £30-40,000 on this item. It was three years in development. It didn't sell. We had the right product. It could do the job. We were selling it in the right places. But we were three years too late.

The market changed from when we started. Back then, everyone was using quarter-pounds. By the time we had the thing developed, everybody was using the bigger tub that held a half-pound. You learn from something like that.

As the company grew, I got another guy to do some selling as well. A younger brother of mine Colm, later joined the company, and also a neighbour, Brendan Moran and my wife Patricia. They were the directors of the company from the start, since 1987.

Over the last twenty years I've done a lot of travelling in Europe, selling products and attending trade shows – always shirts in the press ready to go and a bag with a few bits and pieces in it. But I think I've become more involved with my family. I worked out of home for the first five or six years. I was often on the phone when the kids were small and they'd land in squealing in the middle of a call.

I remember I had a big deal one time with Woolworths for a product. I had the phone in one hand talking to the guy from Woolworths and the next thing one of the children comes in the door crying and I had to catch him by the collar and fire him out and close the door. I didn't get the deal.

As well as getting closer to my family, once the business was up and running I set about educating myself. I did a load of different courses in university: psychology of sales, group dynamics, marketing – anything that was going, I did it. I have a chest of self-motivational marketing books and business books. I had a new urge to educate myself for what I was getting into. I knew that if I wanted to be a professional, if I was going to be the best at what I do, I needed to know all I could about business.

I'm still very limited in qualifications. But there are different types of education. I believe the education of life, of the road, is best. I believe honesty is the best policy. I believe those are the strengths of the company and of me personally. When I do a deal with someone, I complete that deal and honour it the way I said I would.

I've never moved from the west. People ask how could we export because we're not connected to Europe. Sometimes it's an advantage, sometimes it isn't. People in Japan can export all over the world; why can't people from Ireland? We sell stuff to about forty different countries at the moment. We're at all the shows in France, Holland, Germany. We get out there and sell products.

I thought a company, called Volac in Cambridge, a milk replacement company selling product to be fed to calves, should be selling our products, but I was getting nowhere with them.

'Look, the Highland Show is coming up in Scotland,' I said to them after I'd gone over to meet them a couple of times with no results. 'Give me space on your stand. Give me a corner of your stand. I'll give you some of the products and your people will understand when they see the way they sell.'

I got on that stand and I got people to buy the product right there and then. The guys in Volac fell in love with it.

'OK,' they said, 'we'll give you an order.'

So I came home with an order for 150 of the joined-up buckets. A big order at the time.

You have to change people's attitude towards a product made by what they see as a 'Mickey Mouse' company from the west of Ireland that has never been seen in the UK market before. But if you tackle a big market like the UK you must be able to deliver it to them. Once you can do that, you're set.

The last number of years I have made a number of acquis-itions. I looked at a big one recently – a company with a £100 million turnover. We knew the business, understood the busi-ness and wouldn't be afraid, but we walked away because the timing wasn't right. Our biggest development at the moment is probably a £10 million plastic recycling project in Liverpool.

My days are pretty long. In any one month, I could be in the Ukraine for a week, in Prague, and a couple of days in the UK. It's always busy, busy – there's always something going on. Three locations in the UK, a distribution office in Holland, a full manufacturing plant in Poland. Two hundred to 250 people and a €40-45 million turnover. A serious operation.

We are constantly trying to bring in better people. My wife, Patricia, is very involved in the company, doing payments, and my oldest son, Jonathan, is production oriented so when the factory in Poland set up he went out there and got the plant running. It's running successfully and he's now back looking at other things at the moment. Poland for him was a huge challenge. Given the climate change, the cultural change and a serious language barrier, it was a difficult place to start to run a factory and he had limited factory experience in Tuam. But he had the determination and the willpower to meet the challenge.

I'm not a big spender. Money has always been secondary. The primary thing was the company. Building the company. Expanding the company. I always have a five-year plan and anything I've ever written down I've nearly always achieved. I want to go to Sydney Harbour and visit Red Square. Last year we were thirty years married and went on a cruise for the first time. I've seen other people try to build up a company and then raid the company, pulling money out of it to have a lifestyle above and beyond their means.

Your livelihood is the most important thing so you have to make sure that that side of it is right. My own children have to work and earn their own money because that's the way I was brought up. My father and mother were hard workers. At seventeen, it was nothing for me as a truck driver to make two return trips to Dublin from Galway, one after the other. (Of course, today, with the traffic on the roads that's an impossibility – and you're not allowed to drive that many hours.)

But it's not all work and no play. Outside of business, for example, I'm a hot air balloon pilot. I bought a hot air balloon on the web, and then set out to get a pilot's licence to fly it. I would usually do it for charity. I get a great kick out of putting back into the locality, whether it would be a fund for charity events or for anything to benefit local small business. I was one of the first members of the first County Enterprise Board in Ireland and I go back there once or twice a month to talk to start-up entrepreneurs.

'Look at what he did with buckets and a very limited education,' they think, and it gives them a great sense of personal potential.

When I do those talks, I have a suit on, but I prefer to be down on the floor of the factory with the guys in a pair of jeans, and the same way with customers. The only way you can find out what they need is by getting close to them.

Recently, we've got into the business of taking waste bottles, chopping them up into granules and rejuvenating the plastic to go back into full-grade plastic packaging. In the UK market at the moment there's 750,000 tonnes of bottles going to landfill – plastic bottles such as your Coke and milk bottles. Which means there's an awful lot of valuable raw material going to waste. In Europe they would be incinerating it. In some Nordic countries they would be recycling/reusing it and that's what we do. Very successfully. The big plan is to return this plastic back into packaging, in a layered form. In common with all of our projects, there will be a lot of stages involved, from conceiving the idea to designing a product, then designing and producing the tooling, making all the modifications and then taking it to the market place. At that point you come to designing brochures, coming up with the key words that sell the product. All of which involves large numbers of people with different skills and tasks. It's not a one-man show.

I may be the head and the face of this organisation but there's a great team behind me. We have a great team spirit. We get a kick out of what we do – and, of course, out of the social side, too. We never have a Christmas party. Instead, we have a New Year party, pulling in all our people from the other countries. Flights are cheaper at that time. Hotels are cheaper. We have two or three days of sales meetings and they go out fully refreshed into the market place in the middle of January. If we did all of this in December, it would be gone out of their heads by the time they went back to work.

Team-building might sound difficult when we've become such an international organisation, but it works. We have a great relationship with all the UK people – excellent group. The Dutch are great people, as are the Poles.

Probably one of the best traits I have is identifying good honest people. I've also been lucky in the friends I have to consult with, like Pádraic McHale, a very successful business-man I've known all my life, who is a great man to bounce stuff off. I have a brother, Gerard, who has a successful company selling CDs, cash registers and such like, who gives me val-uable insight. The same is true of a younger brother of mine, Colm, who has a brilliant brain. It's important to have people like that with whom you can test out ideas. Overall there is a great team in our company, JFC.

The great advantage these advisers have is that they've been there, done it themselves. Young people today feel that if they're educated, they know more than older people. They're wrong.

There's no way that you can get everything out of books. You need to be involved in the hard facts of life. Being a whiz kid with letters after your name is just the start. You still need to be exposed to the reality of business and of life. You can't do that in college, no matter what degrees they offer. You have to have real-life experience. When you combine good education and real life experience then you have something really valuable.

I always describe myself as 'a farmer gone wrong'. I have a bit of land so if I have to retire, I can go and look after cattle and sheep for a while. I grew up with that. I wouldn't mind doing it again, either. I live on a small farm where I can see cattle and sheep outside the window.

I'm still the same as I was when I was starting out. I still live in the same place with the same people that I grew up with. That's important to me. It's more important than I can express ...

Inside Publishing

Norah Casey, Harmonia

I publish magazines. Some of them are owned by my company, Harmonia. Some we publish, under contract, for other people.

The ones we own are 'consumer brands' and most people know the three women's magazines. Aimed at the younger market, we have *U* magazine, which is very funky. *Irish Tatler* is the oldest magazine in Ireland, launched in 1890. Finally, we have *Woman's Way*, the grande dame of women's publishing in this country. We have Ireland's top women's website called iVenus.com.

In addition to the women's magazines, we have titles like *Diarmuid Gavin's Garden Designs* (launched in 2007), *Food&Wine Magazine*, *Auto Ireland* and *Eat Out*. Essentially, we have a magazine for any stage in a reader's life.

The magazines we publish for others tend to be either customer magazines or employee publications. We also publish *K* magazine for The K Club and magazines for Superquinn and the Dundrum Town Centre. We have a suite of employee titles for the HSE, An Post, Dunnes Stores, Unilever and Dublin Bus.

Harmonia, our overall company name, wouldn't be widely known and recognised in the way the titles of the individual magazines are. Within the industry, however, Harmonia is seen as a company that produces high-quality magazines for different sectors. We do all the work for our own branded magazines and for many of the contract magazines like *Cara*. Everything from editorial concept to commissioning, editing, sub editing, designing, photography, page make-up and zipping pages to PDFs ready for print. The only thing we don't do ourselves is the printing of the publications, which we subcontract to companies in Ireland as well as Spain, Germany, the Netherlands and the UK, selecting which is the most competitive at a given time.

Harmonia's core staff is relatively small: about fifty people. When we're busy we bring in freelance designers and photographers. When we're quiet we have our baseline staff. Not that there are quiet times any more. It used to be that we'd have a quiet time in August and another in January. Now, however, the summer months are really busy. In fact, certain titles work especially well during the summer. *Cara*, for example, because of the number of passengers flying to their holiday destinations on Aer Lingus planes, requires more issues in the summer. *Food&Wine Magazine* is a big summer title, not least because the restaurant awards take place in August when the restaurant trade is quiet. About the only period which is still a reasonably quite time for us is January, so that's when I take my holidays every year.

Growing up, I had no plans to own or run magazines. I had the strangest career path. I left Ireland when I was eighteen to train as a nurse in Scotland. Off I went to wear broderie anglais on my head on the banks of Loch Lomond and succour the afflicted, or so I thought.

The best grounding that anybody can be given in life is being a nurse. Once you've done cardiac massage on somebody at 3 a.m. on your own in a lonely ward, believe you me, you don't dither about making business decisions.

During my early years in nursing, I found that I had a great fear of burns victims. I don't know why. When I was in casualty on my own at night I used to dread the idea that somebody might come in with a major burn. So, to confront it, I went to Bangour, just outside Edinburgh, which is the home of plastic surgery – not to be confused with cosmetic surgery. There, I did a burns and plastic surgery course, confronting it because I was afraid of it. Overcoming my fear, however, and developing that specialist skill was ultimately the reason I ended up leaving nursing. The course also involved plastic surgery for children in later life who had fallen into fires as babies and had facial disfigurements as a result.

I could almost pinpoint the moment when I realised I'd never stay in nursing. It was a night when my patient was a wizened old Scottish guy. He was an alcoholic, living on his own – if you could call it living. He obviously didn't think it was a life worth living, and decided he would end it all. He was addled with beer and wine when he made the decision. In his little one-bedroomed flat, he had a gas heater. So he turned on the gas, but didn't light it. He fell asleep, certain that this would be the end of his miseries. Except it wasn't. He woke up some hours later.

'Ah, sure to hell with it,' he thought. 'I might as well live another day.' He lit a cigarette and the place blew up. It simply blew up around him, burning him grievously.

The odd thing about burns victims is when they come in first they are very lucid, no matter how extensive the damage. The survivability of the damage is assessed by adding up the percentage of the body that's burnt plus the age of the patient. That determines whether they live or die. Children nearly always live, even if they've got 90 per cent burns, because their youth sustains them, whereas older people rarely do, even with lesser damage.

The gas fire explosion meant that this patient in his seventies was quite extensively burnt and had almost no possibility of survival. He was, nevertheless, very lucid. He chatted away to me for about two hours, telling a very sad story about losing his wife and becoming estranged from his children. Then he went into a coma and I specialled him for about three weeks at night time. Every night at eight I went in for the night's work with this silent, tragic old man. I was only twenty-two. The stench in that burns unit was just awful. I thought, 'I really can't spend my life doing this.'

I moved to London to work for the Royal College of Nursing (RCN) as a student officer. Although they had an unfortunate twinset-and-pearls image, they also had a vibrant general secretary whose name was Trevor Clay, who took one look at me and decided, 'Oh, the public face of the Royal College is going to be you, you young thing.'

I was trained to within an inch of my life. I had an intensive one-week course in the BBC in television interviewing and

I had radio training too, plus public speaking training, after which I went out to represent the RCN, making regular appearances on the equivalent, in BBC terms, of *Prime Time* and *Scene around Six*. I could talk on anything. I would just be briefed and wheeled into the studio. I found myself in this job which paid me three times more than nursing. I had a car and a secretary and didn't know what to do with them.

'What on earth am I going to do with my life?' I kept thinking. 'I'm still only twenty-five …'

I went as a postgrad into journalism training in Harlow, at that time one of the four accredited National College for the Training of Journalists courses in the UK. I was writing a lot and many of my family are in media. My sister, for example, is a journalist. Looking back, I realise I was being drawn to the career in which I've ended up. I always feel that nursing was a little detour in my life but I enjoyed it. I loved working in Scotland, I gained wonderful experience, but I found my true calling when I started writing.

That is surprising, in a way, given my background. I grew up in the Phoenix Park where my father was a ranger. My grandfather was active in 1916, together with his brother, and later interned at Frongoch. When he came back he got the job of tending the graves in Arbour Hill. He lived in a lodge in the Phoenix Park, died young after all that shell shock and misery of internment, and my father, who had been working in the Guinness brewery, took over from him.

My father had a great love of writing and reading. In our house, growing up, it was always books. We never had

GALWAY COUNTY LIBRARIES

anything other than books and so he gave us all a great love of the written word, which is my passion.

After journalism training I went to work as a news reporter on the *Nursing Standard*, a weekly magazine for nurses. I was the only person at that time with two such contrasting qualifications – nursing and journalism – which was fantastic for the magazine. It was fantastic for me, too, because I only lasted as a reporter about eight months before they made me news editor. Nine months later I was editor. I ended up being CEO of that company.

I was a complete workaholic. I didn't just do my print journalism. I went on to do television and radio at Ealing. I was doing a PhD at the University of Wales. The magazine company recognised how hungry I was for education so they actually paid a lot of money for me to go to Ashridge Management College to study strategic management.

It was during that course that I really realised just how naive I was. When you take over a managerial role first, you think you know it all. You figure that because you are good at editing you must be great at managing. And of course you're not. It was a real eye-opener for me. I was surprised by how much I loved it. I really couldn't believe that I could have a passion for the spreadsheets and the planning involved in business. Here I was in my twenties, a CEO getting a right kick out of the fact that I could launch a magazine and turn it around or make a business decision that would have an impact on the bottom line.

It was a two-year mentorship programme and part of it was residential. I fell in love with the place to such an extent that

I went back to do another programme at Ashridge a couple of years later and am a lifelong alumni member now. It was a real home from home. Two men there became strong mentors for me and, as my career went on, they were great; they were always at the other end of the phone when I needed advice.

My PhD work at the University of Wales was academic, self-centred and all about me, whereas Ashridge was really about the business and very practical. You went in there to work on something that would have a meaningful result for you and your business.

The publishing company I was running at the time, Scutari (later RCN Publishing), had a portfolio of magazines, an impressive book imprint and a significant conference programme. We also launched *Evidence Based Practice* in association with the *British Medical Journal*, a world-wide standard-bearer in nursing and medicine with the University of Toronto, and when I left it was translated into several foreign languages.

I stayed far too long in that job because I really loved it. There was no limit to what you could do and it was hugely successful financially. I loved the mix of conferences and books and magazines and they all had different paces. I had to make a conscious decision, in 1998, to move on after eleven years, rather than wait and have to be prised out of it. I was so embedded that, to this day, if I turn up in the UK at a nursing conference, the same thing happens.

'Oh God, I know you,' someone will say. 'You're with the nursing and medical magazines.' For all sorts of personal reasons I decided that I would move on and try something different with my life. I went for the *Irish Post*. I wanted to move into mainstream publishing.

The personal reasons arose from the fact that I'd met a BBC broadcaster and married him. I was very keen to cement our relationship with a child. It may be that I stayed so long in my previous job because, when you plan on having a baby, you want to be in a job you feel comfortable in. I knew I could run that company with my eyes closed and it had amazing maternity leave provisions.

But for all my planning, the baby just didn't happen for me naturally. I had to undergo IVF which, as most people who go through it know, is very stressful. My last IVF cycle ended in a miscarriage, which I found very difficult to deal with …

'That's it,' I thought. 'That's it.' I went out and bought a bottle of brandy, and my mother, myself and my husband, Richard, sat down.

'I'm not being good any more,' I told them. 'I'm going to misbehave atrociously. Give me a packet of cigarettes and let me just do whatever I want to do. I need to get out of this job, I need to move on with my life, the world is not going to collapse if I do not have a child.'

Around about the same time, somebody told me about the job at the *Irish Post* and told me I'd be perfect for it. And I was really excited about getting back in touch with my Irishness and working on a newspaper that had such a strong history. I did two interviews and was offered the job. On the day I went to sign the contract I had very bad abdominal pains. I went in to St Thomas' Hospital.

'Well, you will not believe this,' the professor told me.

'Having had four years of IVF you are now naturally, normally, six weeks pregnant.'

I felt honour-bound not to take up the *Irish Post* job without informing them.

'Guys, you know what? I find myself in this embarrassing situation,' I told the CEO of the *Irish Post*. 'I have the smallest little scan of my child at six weeks. I may not be pregnant in six weeks' time. But I should tell you that this is what's happened to me.'

He was great. 'We're with you for the long term,' he said. 'Come on in, see how you get on.' I had a perfectly normal, natural, healthy pregnancy and my little darling miracle boy Dara is now nine.

For most of my time with the Jefferson Smurfit Group (now Smurfit Kappa), which owned the *Irish Post*, I was the only female CEO and I arrived pregnant. They were a great company to work for and not once did they hold me back – either because I was a woman or pregnant. They promoted me three times in the first three years I was with them – the only criterion they judged me on (which is as it should be) was how successful I was at my job and whether I delivered on the figures.

It was radical change on a number of fronts all at once. I had doubts that I'd be able to do it, and from the start I absolutely loved the *Irish Post* and the team who worked there. I joined them as the editor. Editing has always given me the best years in my life, yet I tend to move on quickly from that job. In the case of the *Irish Post*, that happened within a year, because the previous CEO had been planning to move on and did so. I was only back from maternity leave a few months when I took over as CEO. The funny thing I discovered about myself was that while I always had a fanciful notion that I wanted to be editor, actually I was chomping at the bit to be CEO again.

When I was with the *Irish Post* I did all of the big Gerry Adams and David Trimble interviews. I went in at an incredibly exciting time for Irish people in London. The *Irish Post* had a fine history of campaigning for the Birmingham Six and the Guildford Four. It had also gone through some pretty tough times. Of course, coming in at a good time didn't mean readers were passive. They were anything but passive. The editorial stance following the peace referenda was very balanced – taking into account both sides of the divide and playing our part, I suppose, in bridging communities. It wasn't always a popular stance with people who had entrenched views on either side.

I was sent some terrible hate mail, most of which I didn't dwell on but we kept everything on file, just in case. Some of it was sent on to Scotland Yard. Around about the time they had the nail bomber in London, I remember driving home from work, listening to the radio. The commissioner for the London Metropolitan Police was talking about a letter he had received that morning that was very threatening. It sounded a bit familiar and I realised with a shock that I had received the same letter that morning. I was on the phone to them as soon as I arrived home. The worst one came to my home address. We had only recently moved in. I could not believe it. My heart nearly stopped. I woke up one morning and there on the doormat was a letter declaring all sorts of things would happen to me and it was signed with a very well known pseudonym used by a loyalist terrorist group in Northern Ireland. That was pretty frightening – even more so because I had a young baby in the house and I felt it invaded my personal space.

I learned one very important lesson in my early time as editor with the *Irish Post* – stay close to your audience, whatever your own views. Around that time, Cardinal Ratzinger, now Pope Benedict XVI, was firing off encyclicals, one more right-wing than the last. I always felt, as many others did, that he was leading the papal agenda because John Paul II was very ill. After one particularly inflammatory encyclical relating to excommunication and sex before marriage I decided we should do a story on it. Most of the Irish in Britain are Catholic and I felt that this was a strong story that might interest them. We gathered together lots of comments from religious groups and people like Ruth Dudley Edwards.

We ran the story on the front page with the headline 'Pope out of Touch?' which was a quote from one of the commentators. What I did not know at the time, but later learned to my cost, was that a sizeable portion of the *Irish Post*'s sales took place at the back of church on Sundays. So the inevitable happened – as soon as the batches of newspapers arrived at the distributer I got a phone call from him to say the paper wouldn't be stocked at the back of the churches that week.

'It's rather like asking Cadbury's to say chocolate is bad for you,' the distributer pointed out. And he had a point.

It was a great time to be working for the newspaper though and it really brought back into focus my Irishness.

For instance, it allowed me to have something to talk to my father about. From the time I left Ireland at seventeen, when I phoned home my father would pick up the phone and say, 'Your mother wants to talk to you.' Like most dads he wasn't that comfortable with small talk or, indeed, talking on the phone. But he had a great interest in Northern Ireland and during that time I became a bit of an expert on the troubles and the politics of the north and we had some great discussions and debates about the peace process and the establishment of the assembly. He was a great newspaper reader and would keep cuttings from various papers if he thought they would interest me. (He did that for all of us in the family, so he was a busy man.)

Like most businesses we flourished between 1999 and 2001 when the economy was good. We got involved in the FÁS roadshows to help recruit people back to Ireland and it was amazing to see thousands of people turning up at Earls Court waiting to get a job back home – very emotional and a real sign of the times. Smurfits owned a small group of publishing companies and at the time I was CEO of the London company, Smurfit Media, which published the *Irish Post* and did various exhibitions and one-off publishing projects. In 2001 they asked me to also take on the management of the Dublin-based company Smurfit Communications, which published magazines. I commuted for the first year and a half and ran them both.

The commute was interesting. When it started, Dara was eighteen months old. Richard worked in the BBC and it was difficult for him to know if he could be home in time to pick up Dara – he might plan to but if a story broke then he would have to stay for the late news. We had recently said goodbye to our nanny and moved Dara into a Montessori. I decided that the only way I would be willing to commute was if I could take Dara with me so that we would be together as much as possible and he could continue to develop at Montessori rather than go back to a nanny. Looking back I can't imagine what madness possessed me to think that was a good idea but at the time I was determinedly upbeat about it. Every Monday morning we all got up at 4 a.m. and packed the nappies and everything else that goes with a young child (a virtual carload) and got on the plane to Dublin – Dara was great and treated it like a bus journey. We got to know everyone at the airport and on the plane during those eighteen months (the mad woman with the baby). We would arrive into Dublin at about 7.30 and someone would pick us up and drop Dara to the Montessori and me to work – usually I spent the first few hours retrieving bottles and nappies from the briefcase. Then on Wednesday night we went back home again. It was a crazy time.

But what I really loved about spending time in Dublin was getting to be with my family again. I got an apartment close to my sister, who was a godsend, and had a great time rediscovering my city. But the downside, I have to say, is that Ireland was just the most extraordinary market to break into. Everybody would say, 'You must know him. He's married to X. And he's a brother of Y.' I remember making an appointment to meet someone in the Schoolhouse restaurant in Northumberland Road for lunch. As he walked in he was chatting to every table and I thought he must be the most popular person in Dublin.

Of course, after about two months I found myself walking through the same room and doing precisely what he'd done. It's a strange environment of intimacy and networking, compared to London.

In London you go in to a meeting with your presentation, your credentials and a strong proposition. 'I'm great, come and do business with me,' you're saying. 'I'll do a great job for you.'

They will say yes or no and that's the end of the meeting. The first six months here I used to come out on a high, saying, 'I've got that business.' I realised six months later they were trying to be nice and they wouldn't tell me to my face. They didn't really want to see the big presentation; they wanted me to chat and get to know them. It was very frustrating to start with but, four years later, I love that way of doing business and would find it hard to go back to the other way.

I'm in London every week and I have to consciously switch gear on the journey. At times the London way of doing business is very clinical (but it's also clear-cut and safe), whereas in Ireland someone would make a killing if they produced a map of who is related to who and how you actually make connections with people. The other thing I was totally unprepared for was the obsession with which part of the city you grew up in. Thank God I grew up in the Phoenix Park.

'Sure you're not really a northsider,' southsiders would say to me. 'You lived in the Phoenix Park – that's not really the northside.' Northsiders would say, 'You're one of us.' So I couldn't be put in a box.

During that first year commuting between the two cities and learning the complications of business life in Dublin, I

Brian Ranalow, *H&K*

Chloe and James O'Connor, *Stronghold*

Vincent Carton, *Manor Farm*

Colum Butler, *Leisureplex*

Sean Gallagher, *Smarthomes*

Padraigh Ó Ceidigh, *Aer Arann*

Pat Walsh, *Walsh Mushrooms*

John Concannon, *JFC Manufacturing Co. Ltd.*

Ivan Yates, *Celtic Bookmakers*

Norah Casey, *Harmonia*

Kevin Coleman, *GreenCone*

Richard Barrett, *Treasury Holdings*

took over the management of a sister company to Smurfit Communications, iVenus.com. This was a great women's website which was an unfortunate victim of timing with the downturn in online businesses occurring within a year of it being launched. It required a huge amount of effort to reduce the costs rapidly and refocus the business. At the same time, Smurfit Communications required an increasing amount of my time and energy, and three days a week was not sufficient. Something had to give and our home life was suffering too. My husband Richard and I worried fruitlessly for about six months before we woke up one morning and said, 'This can't go on.' Richard gave up his job at the BBC, took a sabbatical and worked for RTÉ for a while. He'd been the health correspondent with the BBC, so he did a ten-part series here called 'The Truth about the Health Service' followed by other series in the same vein. He also did some programmes for BBC Science and started to write again.

He loved the move to Dublin from day one; I was the one who had the transitional problems. Bear in mind that Ireland is 10 per cent the size of the British market, so it is much harder to make money out of volume sales here – especially of magazines that are targeted at a distinct niche.

My greatest success was probably *U* magazine. When I came in first, *U* was almost the same as *Irish Tatler* and *Image*. It was a poor sister, making a negative contribution to overhead – a very poor place for a magazine. It was probably the one we most talked about closing down, because it wasn't a solid brand – it hadn't captured a distinct market and it was hard to distinguish it from the others – which frankly were doing a better job of it. I have always believed, despite many people who told me otherwise, that Ireland is a price-sensitive market when it comes to magazine purchase. Having worked most of my life in London I always kept an eye on what was working over there and, as importantly, through my European colleagues, what was happening further afield. At the time *Heat* was the great success story and had been relaunched in the UK – it was trailblazing in the 18–27 sector with strong celebrity content and a price sensitive marketing drive. In Italy a magazine called *Donna* had launched much in the same vein and had taken the market. As with any business the rules are the same – go in low, steal the market and gradually raise the price and the proposition over time.

The one great thing about Ireland is this extraordinary demographic where we have more young people as a per- centage of population than anywhere else in Europe. So we completely revamped *U* magazine, doing as much qualitative and quantitative research as we could. Our aim was to go down in age profile rather than up. We invested a great deal in the quality of the editorial and production – it was vastly improved, vibrant and cheeky. We trebled the print run and put it out there for a euro. It had one great new addition – we dealt with sex and relationships in a no-nonsense way – and got in to some trouble for doing so. We offended the sensitivities of quite a few rural shopkeepers with our graphic coverlines – most of which I don't think I can repeat here. I remember bringing an issue of *U* to a business meeting (showing off my magazines of course) and one of the cover lines read 'Mickey Mania!'

'Please tell us that's a new pop group,' they pleaded. It was quite different to anything that Ireland had ever produced before. It was bright and vibrant and high gloss. The begrudgers said it wouldn't work, that people wouldn't buy it and that at a euro it was a throwaway.

'You know,' I said at the time, 'time and again people in publishing have proven that even if you charge 50 cent for something, they won't buy it the following month if they think it's trash.'

The low price attracted young readers to try it out, but having tried it out, it was clear, within the first two or three issues, that a great deal of stickiness had built up: people were coming back in again and again. Before we knew it, we had outsold everybody else. The circulation went up to 50,000 in three issues. The price was the introductory factor, but what created the stickiness was great editorial. Many of the Irish magazines at the time were criticised for having poor editorial content. They bought most of the fashion in from London. They didn't demonstrate their relevance to the local market. Because I came from an editorial background, I focused all of my energies to start with on creating great content.

Whether 50,000 or 500,000 readers are buying a magazine, they expect it to look high quality. The bar is high for the British-based glossies like *Glamour* and *Marie Claire*, and Irish magazines have to be in the same zone even though we don't raise as much in advertising revenue. So we transformed the magazine content first and foremost. When we relaunched, the editorial and photography was great, we had fantastic competitions and the whole tone of the magazine was targeted at this very strong niche of young women in their early twenties. In *U*, the language and the style and the tone is you and me chatting, unlike *Vogue* and *Harpers and Queen* where the tone is aloof – like the tone of a coffee table book. *U* magazine, in contrast, offers total engagement. On the other hand, we have a very strong anti-diet policy. This age group are particularly susceptible to imagery and role models and we were conscious of being responsible in light of the increase in eating disorders, in particular anorexia. So we don't publish any material on diets and we tell readers time and again that they should feel comfortable with their body shape and enjoy the way they look rather than trying to change into someone else.

In the magazine business there is a constant turnover of staff. A lot of young people come into the business as a starting point in journalism. I had a fantastic editor who re-launched the magazine with me and is now working for one of the newspapers – she's brilliant. If you get a good editor, you're set. Great design, a great editor, somebody who completely understands the marketing of the title. We were lucky to get another great editor after her and we now have yet another star who helped to relaunch the magazine as a fortnightly this year. When we re-launched *U* magazine, we didn't spend a cent on television and radio. This was all word of mouth.

It proved that young Irish people had radically changed. We might have been coming off the back of an Ireland where people were worried about their pensionable jobs in the bank and the civil service, but this was a completely new generation with different expectations and attitudes.

I had turned *U* magazine around. And then the silliest problem emerged. I found myself with this great magazine every advertiser wanted to be in. But I was turning advertising away because I had chosen to staple it, rather than have it 'perfect bound'. These types of magazines work best when they are stapled – they look edgier than the big heavyweight glossies. The downside is that it limits the size of the publication. Once you go beyond a certain number of pages, the staples come undone. So here's this fantastic magazine and its long-term future is under threat because I can't put more ads into it without it falling apart …

I looked at the *Glamour* size, which is smaller, but quickly found out that younger readers don't like that compact size. Then, going through the research, it struck me. Eighty-five per cent of copies were selling in the first two weeks of the month. Frequency was the issue. Instead of changing the size and keeping the frequency, the solution was to keep the size and increase the frequency. So I now bring it out once a fortnight, not once a month.

Now, of course, we have had a few hairy moments. We distributed free condoms in 2006 with the magazine. We stress safe sex. Every time we talk about sex we say, 'Smart girls carry a condom.' As part of our drive in this sort of territory, we distributed two free condoms at the height of the summer festivals. It was July. It was our smart sex issue. Durex worked with us so we had two free condoms on the front. About five multiple retailers refused to carry it. I phoned Joe Duffy immediately.

'Can I talk to you about something?' I said. 'I'm just furious. You walk into any newsagent and you will see lads' magazines there that are pornographic with lewd topless models. They're just soft porn. Sitting at eye level. Yet these same retailers will not carry my smart sex issue that has two free condoms in it.'

I didn't name them, and all of them by the end of the day had reversed their policy. My point was not to embarrass people, it was to get them to change the way they thought. It was to get them to acknowledge that it was a really good initiative. The fact is that it's young women who carry the condoms. If you look at the incidence of sexually transmitted disease, let alone HIV infection, it's young women who have the power to influence behaviour.

After my rant on Joe Duffy, lots of people phoned the programme, some of whom said it was a disgrace giving away condoms but most of them saw the sense in it. It was great publicity, too, which didn't hurt, but that wasn't the objective.

The next big shift, the one that brought me into ownership, happened in 2004. The Jefferson Smurfit Group was bought by Madison Dearborn, the Chicago-based venture capital company. They were keen to divest themselves of non-core activities. The magazines were definitely non-core and I hoped that there might be an opportunity to do a management buy-out (MBO). I had a really good relationship with the Jefferson Smurfit Group and I really liked working for them so that wasn't the issue – I just think you come to a time in your life when you want to do it for yourself.

The fact is that, even before Madison Dearborn bought them, during the time when I was CEO there was a constant undercurrent of doubt about them being in this business at all – because the business was built around manufacturing, around corrugated paper and packaging. A publishing division sat oddly in the middle of that. So divestment was always going to happen.

It was tough enough, the lead-up to the buyout. The company needed an awful lot of work done to it in the first couple of years after I came back. There were times when I thought I wouldn't actually want to buy the magazines, because they weren't that stable and I had no doubt about the level of energy required to get them to where they could be.

Even at the point of the MBO, I felt like the minister in the old TV series *Yes Minister*, played by Paul Edington. Every time the minister made a bad mistake, the senior civil servant, Sir Humphrey, would say, 'You made a very courageous decision, minister' and it was immediately obvious that he'd made a boo boo. That's all I got with the MBO. People telling me I was very courageous – with the subtext that I might be making a monumental mistake.

It helped that I am totally financially driven, and after all my finance modules at Ashridge I had the ability to do all my own budget forecasts and the all-important cash flow projections. To get comfortable with the legalities, I read everything. I read everybody's case histories. In the two years prior to the MBO, I learned an enormous amount from other people who had done it and got great advice. So by the time I did do the MBO I had a tiny team of people who knew what they were doing and I didn't need to take professional advisers on board.

I felt very comfortable because I knew the business, I am a strong negotiator, I knew what I wanted to get out of it and I am always very conscious that you must always leave something on the table in a negotiation. There's no way that you go into these things believing it's all going to be one-sided.

It was a strange year, though, because of the secrecy. It all had to be done in a very confidential way. I spent ten months worrying about elements of it, then going into the final four months of intensive make-or-break stuff, and nobody, but nobody, in my business could know that I was doing it. Then one great day, when everything was signed, I was free to say, 'I'm buying the business and at this set date in the future I'm going to own it.'

Then, of course, the real work began. There was an enormous amount to do in a short space of time to prepare staff and clients for the change in ownership. The staff were my first priority – in this business the team that works with you is all important and I had a great group of people working with me. Change, even when it's positive, causes a great deal of anxiety, and during those interim weeks my focus was on reassurance and motivation to make sure that the staff put their faith in me and my abilities to run the business successfully. It was steady as she goes in terms of me taking over, unlike the situation where an outside buyer acquires the business and wants to change everything from the outset. It was important, also, to reinforce client relationships – to ensure that key customers felt reassured that I was capable of owning and transforming the business. I have never worked so hard. I didn't take a holiday for eighteen months after the deal.

The great thing about running your own business is that, over time, you get to have all the right people in the right places. We have a great team at the helm. When I did the MBO, in terms of senior management, there was really only me and a relatively new finance manager. We had had some great managers, but as they left, and in the run-up to the MBO, Smurfits quite rightly didn't want to bring in new highly paid managers to replace them.

That proved to be an advantage for me after the MBO, because I could recruit the right people for the right places. They're all bedding in now this year. By the end of last year I wanted to have a full management team in place. I was fortunate because that finance manager who worked with me just prior to the MBO is now our finance director and proved to be one of the best assets that I could possibly have. Our finance team is second to none. I meet other people in similar businesses, who have external accountants or half-time credit controllers, whereas everything in our business is driven by finance so the finance function is invested in and valued.

When I had everything consolidated, it was time to look at the possibility of bringing out new titles. I've spent a year planning a new gardening magazine with Diarmuid Gavin. Diarmuid and I have been talking about doing it for a long time. For me, the most important part of any new launch is market intelligence. We went on a search to find out what other publishers were doing in Europe and internationally in the gardening sector. We also pore over demographic trends and future projections. One of the most important elements of the research phase is the advertisement spend – whether there is enough in the market to take another title or if there are new areas to grow in to.

Diarmuid has such a distinctive design and identity that it didn't take long to find the niche that would work well for us in all of those areas. *Diarmuid Gavin's Garden Designs* is not aimed at gardening enthusiasts, so if you really care passionately about your petunias then this is not the magazine for you. The title is entirely aimed at city dwellers who are probably in their first house in their early thirties, have a lovely garden out the back they don't know what to do with and which they want to look as cool and contemporary as the interior of their home. This magazine is about design, about adding the 'wow' factor with plants and new materials, but essentially it is about inspiring people to be imaginative and creative about their outdoor space.

We've successfully relaunched and repositioned every magazine in the Harmonia stable and my credo is to plan, plan, plan. I work in a sector which is beset by people who believe that it's easy to launch a magazine, and unfortunately they often do – then two months later they're gone and the sector is damaged because of it. So I have to work even harder to ensure that when we launch or reposition that we do it properly – we have solid brands that have stood the test of time and you don't meddle with them lightly!

We're doing well with Diarmuid's magazine and I am really enjoying it, partly because we launched in Britain as well and it's my first little step back. I still stay very connected to London and run fashion shows there. It's also a really important market to us – about 25 per cent of my sales revenue comes out of London and I try to stay really close to those clients and agencies to ensure they remember our little suite of titles over here. It helps that I have a profile in London and I am able to take clients to amazing events – so we punch a little above our weight over there. From my *Irish Post* days I am very involved in the Irish scene in London and I chair the mayor's (Ken Livingstone's) St Patrick's Day festival and sit on the London cultural forum.

One of my great heroes in London is Ken Livingstone. I first met him when I chaired a public meeting in Camden Town when he was a candidate in the first mayoral elections. All the Irish in London wanted me to row in behind him.

'You have to support Ken Livingstone,' they told me. 'He was great to the Irish during the days of the Greater London Council (GLC).'

Of course, that was calculated to get my back up and I thought there's no way he's going to get an easy ride from me. So we were sitting on the panel and every time Ken sniffed they cheered. I kept asking him the most awkward questions and interrupting him and being generally a very difficult chair. He was in the middle of some thing about how great he was and I said, 'Yeah, we've all heard that, what are you going to do for the Irish in London? Come on. Give us some specifics.'

He gave me a very stern look (frankly a bit exasperated, I expect, by my interruptions). 'OK,' he said. 'I'm going to have the biggest St Patrick's Day festival that anybody has ever seen. It will rival New York. I'm going to close the Edgware Road.'

And then, of course, the *Evening Standard* (no fan of his) proclaims, 'Red Ken goes green' and the other right-wing press ran stories about 'Barmy Ken closes London for the Paddies'.

Six months later I got a call asking me to go and see him

to help get the festival off the ground and I ended up running
it for the first few years. I think that first year, when we had
a festival for the first time, it was one of the most incredible
achievements of my life. Remember, if you lived in London
during those years, you didn't necessarily boast about your
background. When there was a bombing in Hyde Park you
kept your head down. Every city had a Paddy's Day festival
except for London, the city inhabited by the largest number
of first generation Irish. A small parade was held every year by
a very courageous group called the Council of Irish County
Associations, and they had kept going through the worst of
times despite getting little or no support.

It took eighteen months to persuade the Conservatives on
Westminster Council to stop thinking that the St Patrick's
Day parade should happen 'up with your own crowd in Kil-
burn' and, even worse, that the streets would not be full of
drunken Irish on the day.

We had big plans. The Greater London Authority (GLA)
under Ken Livingstone had jurisdiction over Trafalgar Square,
and he felt that the festival should be at the very heart of
London. We worked hard with the various neighbours and
partners and organised a great line-up for the stage in Trafalgar
Square. The parade was to leave Westminster cathedral after the traditional St Patrick's Day mass but the authorities
decided that as it was a low-key event they wouldn't close the
roads – how wrong they were.

I remember arriving in Trafalgar Square very early that
morning and the place was obviously desolate, with people
still putting up the last bits and pieces of the stage and stands.

I did a few interviews for BBC London and then went into the backstage area to sort out some last-minute preparations. The next thing, when I looked outside, there was a throng of people waiting to get in. Before we knew it, we had 25,000 people in Trafalgar Square. Down at Westminster Cathedral, where we were only supposed to have 2000 people, another 30,000 had shown up. You couldn't move. It was extraordinary. We upset every taxi driver in London by closing all of the roads because this huge parade was coming towards Trafalgar Square.

By two o'clock, we had 60,000 in the vicinity of Trafalgar Square and we had to close it off. The emotion of that first year was unbelievable. I was standing there at Nelson's column watching the parade coming towards us – this sea of people decked out in green with Irish flags waving, some were crying and hugging. It was a real watershed in terms of how Irish people in London felt about the city – there was such pride and celebration that day. Even the police in London came out with green sashes. In Trafalgar Square, you couldn't move for people and so the whole parade was sent to Buckingham Palace. It was a complete success and the media coverage was uniformly positive.

In the six subsequent festivals, we have never had an arrest. It's a totally family-orientated festival. We've now taken Leicester Square and Covent Garden as well as Trafalgar Square and the parade is properly organised from Park Lane all the way through the centre of London. But that first year is the one I will always remember, because I had never seen such emotion. It was just unbelievable. 'You have done a lot of things but I'm most proud of you for doing that,' is what my mother says to me about it – and she always knows best.

London continues to be a big part of my life. I have a great connection with that city and especially Irish people who live and work there. I just adore living between those two great cities. London is superb at some things Dublin should do more of and Dublin is great at things London should do more of.

In relation to my own business, I could whinge forever about the fact that Ireland has inordinately high postal charges, which almost militates against us growing a subscription business. We also have VAT on the cover price of magazines, whereas there is no VAT in the UK. Not only does Ireland have VAT, it has the highest VAT rate in Europe on magazine sales.

We are also unfortunate enough to live next to an English-speaking neighbour who floods the market with its own titles. There are no barriers to entry so it is really easy to print a few thousand more for the Irish market. The problem that poses is that even if a title sells only one copy, it's going to take up the same shop space as mine.

Magazines are also susceptible to the economic climate. On the plus side, cover sales go up during a recession. Women will buy more magazines; they can't afford to go to the hairdresser or the spa but they'll buy the magazine to have that little bit of luxury – I often think that the women's magazines in particular offer a little bit of escapism, they're inspirational and fun. On the downside, our advertising sales diminish when times are tough – especially in the luxury goods market.

It's so hard at the moment to get a read on where the market is going – we're not involved in property investment but any downturn in that sector will have an impact on us. I hope that perhaps investors will look at sectors other than property now – particularly my own, of course.

Each publication from Harmonia is exposed in a different way to a market downturn. *Woman's Way*, for instance, is not that exposed on advertising because it earns its keep just on cover sales, whereas *Irish Tatler*, like all monthly glossies, which sell fewer copies, is more exposed on sales because it attracts advertisers selling to the high end of the market. By increasing the frequency of *U* it is now less exposed on advertising because cover sales are much higher. In the business overall we keep a very balanced portfolio – on the contract side we concentrate on employee and customer magazines, which are solid and should continue to see strong growth in coming years. With iVenus.com we are hoping to tap into the steep growth in online sales revenues.

We have an €8 million annual turnover and the best way to grow that is through acquisitions or launches. I would love to grow through acquisition, maybe in the British market; there is a very limited amount available in Ireland.

I am still a bit of a workaholic. We're usually up about 6.30. Dara goes to school at St Conleth's so I have until 8.30 with him before we drop him off. By contrast, evenings are really bad (we've been very busy, so I am not complaining too much). But I used to have it under control – generally I went home at 6 p.m. and had a couple of hours with him before bedtime – once he was asleep I was able to put the computer on again and work away. But now I am staying later and later at the office – I have given myself a stern talking-to recently and I am determined to do something about that. Everyone else appears to be cracking the work–life balance thing at the moment so I really should catch up.

My problem is that I usually say yes to everything. At this particular moment in time I'm carrying two lots of proofs around that have to be signed off, I've a big tender presentation in a couple of hours and a brainstorming on a new event we're planning next year. Publishing is always a bit manic – it never slows down. Sometimes I get a great kick out of it and I think, 'This is the best thing I've ever done in my life' and other days I just drag myself out of bed and think, 'Oh my God, why don't I go into flower arranging or something?'

I finally wrestled Richard (my husband) away from the BBC and he is now the editorial director in the business. It's fantastic to have him there, he's hugely talented and great to work with – it's made a big difference to the business. I rely enormously on him and the finance director, Michael.

Richard and I met at a media dinner after he had spent weeks covering the trial of Beverly Allitt, the nurse who had Munchausen Syndrome by proxy. He was completely exhausted and, I thought, incredibly funny. Then we spent a whole year pretending that the BBC and my company ought to be very close, which allowed us to have business lunches and meetings. We didn't so much as touch or shake hands, and then one fateful night he lunged for that kiss …

Neither of us pushes Dara into anything. He is a relaxed child who is comfortable with himself. I just want him to have as happy a childhood as I had. I was one of six, a middle child sandwiched between two brothers – and of course a tomboy. Not only did we live in the most incredible place, but my sense throughout my childhood was of having both my father and mother around the whole time. My dad sadly passed away a few years ago and tore a hole in all our lives – he was an incredible man who influenced us all. My mother is still alive and she is the most amazing woman. If she's not in New York, she's in Paris or shopping (a trait I definitely inherited from her). She lives life to the full and is a pleasure to be with.

I think all of my brothers and sisters would agree that our parents never forced us to move in a particular direction – they encouraged us to be ourselves and to enjoy life. We all have that capacity. Parents can be overly focused on their children's lives today – maybe it's because we invest so much in them and their future. I would like to think that we will continue to allow Dara the space to choose whatever path is right for him; if it's magazine publishing then that would be great, but we would both be just as happy if he ends up a drummer – which is his current ambition!

The Fun of the Deal

Colum Butler, Leisureplex Group

My Dad said to me at twenty-two years of age, 'If you don't put your head on the block you may not be in a position to reap the reward. You have to put your head on the block because that's what risk and reward is all about.'

Partly because of that advice I wanted to work for myself, to lead a team to take the risk and earn the reward. When I found myself aged twenty-one, qualified as a chartered accountant, I had no doubt that I wanted to be doing things for myself, setting up companies, taking a risk, rather than sitting in an office environment advising people. So I started in the snooker business given that I had worked as a student in my Dad's snooker club to earn a penny over the years.

I started off with an agency for snooker tables, which together with exposure to snooker halls gave me a taste for the emerging leisure business. I, together with a wider consortium, bought Dundrum Bowl in 1987 and the origins of Leisureplex came into being. We opened a second unit in Coolock in 1992. For a while I was tied as a finance director but I yearned for general management and independence. In 1992 I bought out the Dundrum and Coolock business with my brother, Ciaran.

Six weeks after the purchase, a major storm flooded the entire centre, filling the basement of 10,000 sq ft with water seven feet deep, flooding the car park and my wife's car. It was frighteningly sudden. Water came in the basement windows, where staff were working at the time, although no customers had arrived, fortunately, since it was only half eight in the morning. Thankfully, there were no injuries.

We were fortunate to have proper insurance cover, and that, in turn, allowed us to buy a company called Leisureworld. Leisureworld had bowling centres in Cork and Tallaght almost identical to Dundrum and two in the north of Ireland (which we sold on virtually immediately). They were a perfect remodelling opportunity for the Leisureplex brand.

It helps that I am in business with my brother Ciaran, who, like me, qualified in accountancy straight from school. We see eye to eye, but at the same time we beat each other up on ideas and strategy and tactics all the time. When together we have a board meeting every five minutes. When he goes on holidays the 'ideas' side of my brain gets a real holiday, and vice versa. Each of us gives the other's brain a rest. But the great thing is to be with someone who is as involved, who shares the exact same interest in the business, who thinks strategically and tactically. If it was a game of chess, put the pair of us together and the opponent on the other side would have a difficult job because we think a few moves ahead, we're playing with all the 'what ifs', we come up with quirky different angles as to what the other guy might be at. This has given us the ability to complete deals other people can't.

Because we believed that Leisureplex had the ability to become a recognised brand or franchise, we added the Stillorgan Bowl to our business in 1996. At the time it was owned by a family who had built it in 1962 at a capital cost of €62,500.

Buying a family business is always complicated. A key factor in doing a deal is identifying the real decision maker. In this particular case we nearly lost the deal until we eventually realised we had to match grey hair with grey hair. The matriarch of the family (and a medical doctor), a very smart lady indeed who was seventy plus, was the person we needed to win over. My father, an experienced businessman, played a critical part in the negotiations with the matriarch.

In 1997 we built Leisureplex Blanchardstown, and in the process we created a property portfolio. Understanding the values of freeholds and leaseholds, we always wanted to hold onto the freeholds, and in Anglo Irish Bank we had a great supporter.

Leisureplex by now consisted of five units – four around the M50 and one in Cork. We started to invest heavily in maintenance, upkeep and presentation. I was always obsessed with standards and with tight financial control. In addition, however, a huge part of what helped us progress was that we had people developing along with the business. We have never lost one key person. All our senior team are with us for years. Having the same people in a business makes it so easy, because they know your ways, you know their ways and trust is a huge part of the relationship.

A by-product of our leisure and entertainment business was food, and we decided to focus on it. In the restaurant business, if you lose your experienced people you can't maintain consistency, sustain margins, you can't get the training up to the level you need to have by way of service – service with a smile, service with speed. It takes a long time to get all of those going. The first six months in any new unit are the most difficult given the time it takes to put all systems in place. It is unfortunate for any new service establishment that it is in these early days that the critics arrive, ready to judge your performance. That performance is only going to be good if the place is staffed with experienced team members; in the early days when you are still recruiting, the experience simply is not there – time in turn helps to cure this issue.

I for one will not seek to criticise a new service establishment within its first six months of operation – I will simply not go there for the first six months. One advantage of growth is that you develop experienced staff who can be decanted into new openings – achieving higher standards earlier than six months after a new opening remains our challenge.

The food component of our Leisureplex business went from 5 per cent of turnover to nearly 20 per cent in the first ten years of operation. We brought in experience – a lady (still with us) with vast UK experience. She knew the science behind the restaurant business. She moved over here, bringing the science of how to profit from food. I believe any business is easy if you understand the science behind that business.

In the restaurant business, the science lies in how you get someone to buy a particular steak or side order by how you dress it up and present it, together with constant attention to detail on cost of sale/stock control/margins. Whether you highlight an item in a particular way on the menu – as in 'new', 'special' etc – then you can lead the customer to purchase particular items, helping you to achieve a targeted gross margin. By using marketing prowess, presentation and good graphics you can influence the choices people make. Controlling costs in detail through the use of current cost control systems is fundamental.

People's food habits were changing at this time, too. They were eating out more. When we were building Leisureplex Blanchardstown we put a restaurant unit in front. We had our eye on the TGI Friday's franchise and believed that if we had the right properties we could secure the franchise – the Blanchardstown property was a perfect fit. We became the sole Irish franchisee for the TGI concept in 2001. In securing most business deals, an introduction is essential. We realised it was critical to get an introduction to the top people on the other side with a strong reference. If a contact of yours can introduce you to the top people, they're more likely to decide you're worth meeting and worth meeting quickly. KPMG helped us with this introduction.

Using TGI Friday's to extend the food side of our business, we set up restaurants in Blanchardstown, Stephen's Green, Blackrock and Dundrum. As we progressed, we were able to take core systems and experience from the existing restaurants. We opened Dundrum and hit the ground running because we had a team of people who knew what they were doing. I have observed a crucial point of risk in the food business.

It happens when operators who run one restaurant open a second one. Very few people can make that critical transition. They can operate one restaurant to a high standard by being there themselves, but they can't run two successfully as it is simply not possible to be in two locations at the same time. It rarely works.

Our success is that our systems can be in two places at the same time!

What distinguished us from our competition was a dual advantage. The first was that we picked the right people and retained them. The second was that we have an enormous respect for systems. Because of my accountancy background, I would obviously place a high priority on good systems of financial control. But it goes much further in our operation. We understand systems, we understand how to implement, how to get delivery. We were able to invest in developing systems because we were big enough to spend money and throw people at developing the systems. The first year in food we made no money. I wasn't expecting to make any money. I laugh when I see some business plans suggesting how much money they're going to make in year one. Making money in year one in any business is an exception!

We were arguably the leaders in the operation of franchised casual dining restaurant brands in Ireland. Owning and operating a chain of franchises doesn't attract the same admiration that setting up your own business from scratch does, but in fact it's more challenging because you have to meet extraordinarily high standards while nestling the franchise into a context that couldn't be more different to the context out of which it grew. You have to take a series of procedures, do them excellently, yet interpret the franchise so it speaks to the Irish market place.

The American franchise restaurants have really fantastic kitchen systems. You walk into the kitchen in Friday's, you look at table five and it's counting down from the time that the starter left the waiter's deck and went out to the restaurant. It's counting down, indicating the main course is due on that table in seven minutes because that's the average time they'll take to eat their starters. It's that precise.

We have a stable of franchises with Hard Rock Café in Temple Bar, Outback Steakhouse in the UK and now Starbucks in Ireland. We opened our first two Starbucks in Blanchardstown. We have also created a different restaurant concept ourselves called Dantes – a typical Pizza Express-type offering. We have opened Dantes in Dundrum, Blackrock and Blanchardstown.

GALWAY COUNTY LIBRARIES

Our systems can accommodate these businesses, and our staff are set up for that kind of operation. If you take on something that doesn't fit your systems it can take disproportional time, whereas if you incorporate an operation that does fit your systems, the path to growth is a whole lot simpler and 'controlled'.

When we have ventured outside Ireland, we have done so with the wariness drawn from success on the home front. That has driven us to ensure we always have a local partner. In Dublin, you can figure out pretty quickly that there's a certain side of the road you must be on to do business successfully. One side of Dawson Street, for example, is a safe bet: your business will fly; cross to the other side of the street and you may struggle.

Now, if you bring me over to the UK, into Birmingham or any of the big cities, and tell me 'this is the road to be on', how do I really know whether it's the right or wrong side? I don't. So you must have a good local partner. Even then, the plcs don't rely on the local guy. They put teams out with clipboards to establish precisely how many people walk past the door; using maths and science they select the right locations.

Through the years we made other non trade-related investments – investment properties, residential land, equities, financial derivatives – which has resulted in a broad portfolio of assets. We are constantly scouting for opportunity – opportunity that bolts on to or grows our trade with perhaps a spin-off to enhance the asset portfolio side.

We recently bought the UCI cinema business given that its properties were freehold and the business could easily bolt on to our systems, resulting in a broadening of our property portfolio and an enhancement to our trades. We had a Leisureplex unit right beside UCI in Coolock, right beside UCI Blanchardstown and down the road from UCI in Tallaght. We could see the synergistic possibilities, including the immediate retail potential and the longer-term property value. UCI Tallaght was the beneficiary of a property play due to the redevelopment of its car park. Following the acquisition, we sold off these rights.

We used our knowledge and expertise to great effect on that transaction and realised our exit on our Tallaght site almost immediately at a significant premium. It was a demonstration of how clear we are on every process – we knew the area and we knew our advantage.

That clarity is easy when you have two partners/brothers with complementary skills and total trust in each other. Those factors facilitated our getting into highly sophisticated financial derivative work. That aspect of our business is demanding – but also fun. It's good brain-teasing stuff, which comes out of Ciaran and I rubbing off each other, coming up with an idea, arguing it out and then actually making the idea happen.

Because we are two brothers in business together we need to be careful where this overlaps into family life. We could constantly be in discussion teasing out details of prospective deals, so we have to consciously protect other aspects of our lives. We have to switch off the Blackberry at 7 o'clock when we go home in the evening. That, to me, is critical.

I'm constantly busy, but it's not because I'm a control freak. I remember years ago having a conversation with a man who really admired the workaholic lifestyle. He felt the admirable figure was the one who was always out there looking for a deal, who was ego-driven, ever ready to trample on people. I found myself talking about the need for a truly balanced life. Come seven in the evening, every evening, my Blackberry is switched off. I deliberately don't have my Blackberry and telephone on the one machine because I like to manage my personal and business time, rather than have incoming emails manage my time for me. That's particularly important when you run a business that is not nine to five.

Some of our locations have an interesting mix of neigh-bours, some of them from the old inner city, some of them new Irish. It has been suggested, for example, that there may be more guns in Blanchardstown than anywhere else in the country. Add to that locational challenge the fact that, on the face of it, a Leisureplex location could represent a drug pusher's paradise and you will understand that we're not just in the leisure business, or the food business, or the franchise business or the property business. We're also in the risk management business. That requires us to understand all of the implicit risks, train our staff to cope with them and maintain a strong relationship with the authorities.

I suppose the best illustration of how competent our people are in a frequently challenging situation is provided by the traffic on my Blackberry and on my mobile phone. On the Leisureplex side of things, because it's grown and the competence and confidence of our people have grown at the same time, I rarely get a phone call because the problem will be dealt with on the ground. When I turn my Blackberry on in the morning, I'll get messages updating me, but, significantly, not seeking action or intervention from me. Of course, everybody has my home number but they wouldn't ring it unless there was an unprecedented problem requiring my involvement.

It sounds great when I say I turn off my Blackberry when I go home at night and don't really answer my mobile, but of course turning off the technology doesn't turn off my mind. At any hour of the day or night, my mind is still rattling on, looking for the opportunity angle, never really switching off. Without intending to, I am terribly observant. Today, I might notice a paint chip on a ventilator grid. I'll file away the information without even knowing I've done it. Then, if tomorrow I notice there are two chips on the ventilator, I begin to wonder why that has happened.

I'm all the time taking in too much detail. That is a positive in many ways but stressful in others. In order to get balance in my life, I have to find ways to remove myself from the detail. When I go home in the evening, I go for a shower and when I come out of it, the mobile is off and everything is off and then I'm totally present with my wife, kids and friends. No business.

We are incredibly lucky with where the country has got to, really, where we can all prosper. I don't think we're great at celebrating what we can and do achieve. There's an Irish mentality that keeps looking for the bad times even in the good times. It's a dreadful Irish trait, but it exists and feeds into what's sometimes thought of as begrudgery.

We've had great exposure to the Americans, these multi-billionaires who started magnificent companies, for whom life is just one big play centre. They're fascinating to watch, with their jets and their ex-wives and their kids here, there and everywhere. How they keep it all going I just don't know. It's fun to watch, when we're in the United States, but I don't admire what they stand for.

What I really love is that at this point in my life – I'm forty-five years of age – I have a list a mile long of businesses, projects, ventures, plans we're engaged in. Not only do we understand all the different parts of those ventures, but we have a very solid business so it's more enjoyable today because our risk is relatively low.

The other thing I really enjoy is that the team has stayed

the same. Directly around us within head office we have never lost anybody – ever. Most of our key people have been with us a seriously long time, or were with us at one phase, briefly left us, and have come back to us.

There is a great informality about the group. Our style is very relaxed. However, we are quite formal about results, goal-setting and standards-checking. We have mystery guests coming in and out of our different units who give them points for this and points for that. We have great pride in what we do, in being better than the competition, in having good systems, good communication.

We insist on weekly management meetings at local level. Organisations that don't have regular meetings tend to disintegrate. Nascent disagreements, unaddressed, fester. Minor problems, untackled, become major difficulties. Everybody's problem gets solved with communication – no doubt about that. That's one of the driving beliefs behind the company. I should be so approachable that anyone working for us – I don't care where he is, who he is, what part of the group he's in – should be able to come up and talk to me and raise an issue with me, and I should be able to go up and talk to them. Communication is key for us.

The people I admire have high morals, have strong values and achieve a good balance between business and family. Take, for example, a man like Bernard McNamara, who you can sit down and do business with on a handshake, without the need for paperwork because there's so much trust between the two sides. Similarly, I admire Sean FitzPatrick and find him easy to deal with, because he is very good at motivating and bringing people on; he's a super achiever and a very good judge of people. I'd look up to people like Sean and Bernard, but I wouldn't look up to the sharks at all. I like people who have good values. You are always able to do a deal with them and you know you'll both work it out if there's a trouble spot.

When I was growing up I saw business people who treated others so badly that employees would turn into work shivering, scared of what might happen to them next. Any manager who behaves like that has no understanding of people – of himself or of others. I always preach that everybody is the same. Just because someone has a title, he's no better than you are. You should be able to go up and shake his hand and not be intimidated.

When people ask me how I relax and if I have a favourite sport, the honest answer is that work is my favourite sport. Work is like a hobby when you're allowed do it at your own pace and your own time, whereas it's stressful when other people are pulling out of you and trying to drag you in different directions and make you do things. I do feel stressed if I'm out of control, if I don't feel I have my finger on all the pulses.

What I do is I decant my brain into the laptop, build up a lot of information and say, 'if I can get that into the laptop, I have it and I don't have to remember it.'

Information management and people management – they're the key issues. Today, we probably have about 1,400 people working for us. But the numbers are not the defining factor. No matter what your scale of operation, in my view people are the issue. People are always the issue. Most issues you have in business are people-related.

The inability to close down my mind follows me everywhere. Even on holiday, when I play the golf course, I find myself wondering if the golf course is for sale. It's never about the money. It's about the fun of the deal.

I love being successful within a team of people and them becoming successful. Going into Leisureplex in Blanchardstown and from there to Friday's in Blanchardstown on a Saturday and seeing the place hopping, the staff hopping, the manager in good form – everything is good because they're all doing so well. I get real satisfaction there. That, to me, is a real buzz.

I've no interest in drinking. I never developed a taste for it – probably because of working by day and then studying by night during the college years and then getting married very early. Not drinking, for me, is not about being in control – I simply do not like the taste of alcohol. I love company, though. I love being around other people. I enjoy the one-to-one conversations. And I get great relaxation out of music. I play a few instruments and I do that late at night on my own when I can turn up the amp.

So Dad, I guess I put the head on the block a few times – but it's been fun and, so far, no one has managed to chop it off.

Centuries in the Chicken Business

Vincent Carton, Carton Chickens

We're a very old family business. I run it with my brother and we are the eighth generation of Cartons in the business. We go back to 1775.

Our forebear started a livery stable right beside the fruit markets in the Smithfield area of Dublin. He minded the horses for the shopkeepers who came in with their horses and carts. They would come in from far-flung places like Baldoyle and Lucan and Clonskeagh ...

While he was taking care of the horses, he watched what the shopkeepers were buying. They went to the fruit markets for their fruit, they went to the fish market for their fish and they went up the road to the meat market for their beef. But the one thing that wasn't available was poultry. He decided to get into the poultry business. In those days, remember, we were under British rule, so he needed a poulterer's licence from the Crown. So we have in our possession still our original poulterer's licence dated 1807.

At that time, all the farmyards of Ireland had chickens

running around. When Carton started up his business, those farmers would kill their chickens and put them on the trains. We would collect them from the stations around Dublin and bring them to a market we had created where shopkeepers could come and bid. The same system developed into the Christmas turkey market; we ran that as well. Oh, and don't forget rabbits. Basically rabbits were seen as vermin on a farm. They ate crops, so every schoolboy in the country was sent out after school to snare rabbits. Then they needed some way to get rid of the rabbits so they did the exact same thing as they did with their chickens. They put them on the train.

Isn't it amazing? Imagine a chap down in the west who doesn't know me or Cartons or anybody but on trust puts his rabbits onto the train with a little ticket with his name on it, to be collected by Cartons. At Heuston station our chap picked them up off the train and brought them to our market where they were auctioned off. In the case of the rabbits, local butchers would have bought them, taken them home, skinned them and hung them up for sale in the shop. We would take our commission and send the postal order back down to wherever it was – west Clare, Mayo, Kerry, anywhere.

Trust and word of mouth … that's something you can do when you've got an old family name, that's the sort of tradition that builds up. That's what we did and obviously it wasn't in our interest in any way to break that bond of trust so we maintained it. The word spread. We got more supply. We could sell more. It was perfect.

Apropos trust, we have an interesting parchment on the wall of our lobby, going back to famine times. What people don't realise is that back in the famine the cities were every bit as much affected as the countryside. We all know about the blight hitting the potato. People on the farms had their crops rotting in the fields but, at the same time, people in the cities were also buying potatoes and that was their basis of living, so when the famine hit in 1841 and again in 1842, 1843 – year after year – people in the cities started to die.

As they died in far greater numbers, the bodies weren't being collected, so the water table of Dublin was being polluted by the putrefying corpses. At that stage, our base of operation was just north of Smithfield fruit market – a place called Linen Hall. It's a very old part of Dublin. My forefather, Denis Carton, had a farm out in a place called Poppintree, where IKEA is about to build its new superstore. Back then it was a farming area and Denis Carton had a springwater well on it. So what he did was – every day during the famine years – bring fresh water from that well for the people of Linen Hall. We have a parchment hanging in our lobby expressing the thanks of the Lord Mayor and people of Dublin from that time.

It was rabbits that gave us one of our first major crises. I remember my dad telling me that in 1956 we were a very very big player in the game market. Rabbit stew was a big thing in Ireland at that time. Overnight, myxomatosis struck. He remembers one week we were doing hundreds and thousands of rabbits per week and the next week nobody would touch them because of the disease. The roads were littered with dead animals. So that, effectively, was the end of the rabbit market.

But it was in the 1950s that the chicken market really

changed, because of the kinds of chicken being produced. Up to that point, it was boiling fowl all year round. Boiling fowl were the hens – spent hens as they called them – that were tough and needed boiling before they were edible. That was the standard, except for six weeks, when a thing called a spring chicken came on stream. It was, as the name implies, the fresh progeny coming through at springtime.

Then the Americans invented the broiler chicken, which effectively allowed spring chicken to be available all year round. They recognised that if you brought the hens and the cockerels indoors, they would supply eggs all year round. Nature had chickens laying only in spring so that the young chicks would hatch at the best time for them to develop, which was springtime.

By bringing them indoors, they could produce the perfect conditions all year round so they produced eggs consistently throughout the year and spring chickens all year round.

That pumped potential into our business that hadn't been there up to that point. Into our chicken business, that is. Because by the 1970s we'd got into a lot of other businesses, like butter, wine, imported tinned fruit and tea. Except that Ireland was now going into the EU and all of these businesses needed to improve their standards, so basically it was either invest or get out. As a family, we chose to invest. We built a new factory in Co. Cavan in 1970 to be ready to meet the standards of the EEC as it was then in 1973. We chose one business and sold off everything else. Chicken was chosen because it held the most profit potential, to be straight about it.

All of the other businesses were becoming specialised. If

you think about the butter business, that was clearly going to be the creameries. The whiskey business and wines and spirits were also becoming more specialist. We were just a general trader in all of them. A jack of all trades. We were also in the cash and carry business – we had three cash and carrys as well – which was too small when you saw the way the chains were building up. We had a load of these little businesses, so we said, 'Right, where can we make a significant difference?'

By investing in the plant in Shercock in Co. Cavan, my father created a brand new facility with the standards that would meet EU recognition, and within the next five years, five or six of the major players disappeared out of the business.

Chicken distribution means a lot of small items to carry, and transport costs are critical. So the idea was to bring the processing base closer to our chicken farmers and also closer to the ports from which we carry the wheat and grains to feed them. Being close to the chicken farmers means that you can call on birds quickly as the market dictates and, secondly, you can reduce your transport costs, which is what we did. Every time the price of oil goes up it hurts us like hell.

From the time I was a kid, I was mad keen to get into the family business. I joined after doing a B. Comm. in UCD with the intention of changing the world and I very quickly found that it was a very old, very traditional and very what I would describe now as an uptight business. It wasn't modern, it wasn't flexible. And even though my father at that stage controlled 50 per cent of it, I made the decision to get out, study hard and become a management accountant. I joined the company in 1980 but left again in 1983, having got my qualification, and went to Mullingar where I joined Penn, the tennis ball company. It was magic education because I learned all about American company accounting controls which are superb – absolutely superb. Then I got engaged, so I came back to Dublin and took a job with the company that is now Eagle Star, before I got the opportunity to buy back into the business. My brother and I reorganised the operation so it's now 50:50 – the two of us running the business.

What brought me back was the sudden death of my father's cousin who controlled the other half, and who just invited me back in to the business. I think he was impressed that I'd gone off on my own. He liked the idea that here was a Carton doing something all by himself. Unfortunately he died even before we could actually execute the deal, but three years later his widow did, so I got to buy his shares, which were controlling shares at the time.

Basically we leveraged the ownership of the business on the extra performance of the business. Effectively the company provided the money for me to borrow to buy shares. We then bought all other shareholders out, which meant we now had a clean capital structure.

One of the reasons why this company is still around after eight generations is that control has always passed to one or two people rather than fragmenting the shareholding. So even after two hundred years there were only two people really to sort out in terms of the controlling shares – my father and his cousin.

It doesn't sound fair but that's what actually happened. And it worked. When Justin (my younger brother) and I started to plan what we were going to do, because we had heard plenty of history of prior generations getting the management of the business wrong, we knew exactly what the pitfalls were. Even though there was a 50:50 split, we all agreed one or other of us would be the managing director. He's been MD in the past and I am now. We were both adamant that we'd never work against one another, that we'd always aim at doing the best for the company, that we wouldn't get into ego, that there was going to be no sides to this. Each of us has a function and we've got to perform that function, leaving ego outside the door. That's what's actually happened over fifteen years. It's worked out well.

It helps that we rarely disagree because we actually see the world from exactly the same spot. He has his expertise – very much so – in the whole IT area. He's done some amazing stuff for the company in terms of traceability, which is now the buzz word in food. He put it in years ago. He was way ahead of his time on the technical side of things. We wanted to compete with foreign chicken and we weren't allowed to put the word 'Ireland' on it – that's law. EU law says you're not allowed label the country of origin on your product. So he came up with this idea: suppose we put the farmer's name and address on it? So rather than say 'Ireland', we could say 'Co. Monaghan'.

Chicken farms today may have four or five chicken houses on them and that's all controlled by computerisation. He literally computerised our entire chain, from breeding farms to the hatchery; from the feed mill to the growing farm and the final processing plant where it's labelled. From that label we can work all the way back, which became extremely valuable in terms of marketing ourselves to supermarket groups.

We own the hatching, the feed mill and the final processing plant and there's a reason for that. For every euro that we invest in processing, milling and hatching, the farmer needs to spend a euro in chicken housing and stock, effectively. So the coordination of all concerned is crucial.

The reason we control the hatchery is because that's the supply of the numbers of chickens that we need in any week. That's extremely important to us. The feed we control, because if you look at all the problems that have occurred in the chicken or any of the animal food business, the feed is the one area where things have gone wrong. Salmonella, dioxin, foot and mouth disease or even influenza – all of them come through the feed. I often say to supermarket groups that I'm actually selling insurance, not just food. I'm not going to blame anybody else. I'm responsible for every chicken and everything that chicken is eating. And, I can show you the full records and all the tests we've done to make sure that is a premium quality product.

Feed is primarily grain – 65 per cent wheat, 25 per cent soy bean, while rape seed, barley and other grains form another 5 per cent. Then, on top of that we use fish oil and salmon oil. We use vegetable oils as well. Birds preen a lot so they need the oil. Then there's calcium and there's some enzymes that help the bird digest the grains in the feed.

The one medication we give is coccidiostat because, just as dogs have worms, chickens have a little parasite that will live in the gut of the bird and literally has the same effect as distemper would have in dogs, so we must protect the bird against that – it would be cruel not to. That's why we use coccidiostat – it's the only form of medication that's in our mill.

We use no hormones, and no antibiotics. Antibiotics are used elsewhere simply because, back in the 1950s, in the States in particular, they wanted to give a balanced diet to a bird, a pig, a cow, a sheep – whatever. They came up with the idea of grinding down all these various grain sizes – maize and wheat and soy beans – into a powder and then sticking them all back together in a pellet shape with steam and pressure. It was brilliant in that every bird would get a balanced diet of vitamins and carbohydrates and so on.

The problem was that a chicken cannot eat pellets. Its system is designed to break down wholegrains. The pellet went straight into its gizzard, where it was macerated and digestive juices added. It very quickly just fell apart and became a Weetabix-type mixture that went into the small intestine. Insufficient time in the gizzard meant it wasn't acidic enough. Unfortunately, its ph was such that it was the perfect medium for a condition called scour (diarrhoea in humans).

The boffins came up with the answer: antibiotics. Antibiotics in the pellet, so it would kill the scour bacteria and enable the bird to absorb the food and pellet. Great. Except it missed out on a fundamental point about the bacteria. In one month, a bacterium goes through the same number of generations as mankind has to date. It has learned to mutate and to change and become immune to the threat of antibiotics. So let's say it was resistant to a salmonella bug and the consumer ate chicken that had been fed pellets with antibiotics, got salmonella, and their doctor prescribed antibiotics. They wouldn't work, because the bacterium has learned in the gut of the bird to live with antibiotics.

Our milling engineer came up with the brilliant idea of milling only two thirds of the grain. The last third, unmilled, consists of whole grains. You can actually see them in the pellets. Those whole grains enter the gizzard of the chicken, force it to work hard and produce loads of digestive juices, and we don't need to use antibiotics – haven't since 1996. We never used hormones and now they're banned in the EU anyway.

They still use antibiotics and hormones in the United States. We've a great tradition of taking the best and rejecting the worst of American poultry production ideas. One example is the chicken house system.

The manager of a feed mill owned by Pattons in Monaghan town, named George McLean, back in the late 1940s and early 1950s brought a group of young farmers from the outlying area over to America and showed them these chickens that were all the year round spring chickens and how they could be produced. They then came home and started the first wave of production. That is the reason why Monaghan today is the most intensive poultry producing region.

McLean wasn't interested in marketing the product. He was a feedmiller so he was selling feed to these farmers. But they needed to sell their chicken so they came down to the Dublin market, and who was running the Dublin market but us. All of a sudden they had spring chickens outside of spring. So that was a big sell at the time. All through the 1960s the business grew and grew and in 1962 we set up a processing plant just north of the fruit markets in Dublin, moving out of it in 1970.

Each of the farmers who supplies us would usually have about four chicken houses with 25,000 in each, so 100,000 would be the average size. We have ninety farmers. The birds will live for thirty-five days before the females get killed and the remaining ones will get killed before forty-five days. We also have twenty-five breeder farms. They help both males and females mature, get together and produce fertilised eggs for our hatcheries.

Plus we've a feed mill feeding both. Back in 1974, Thos P. Carton (T.P. as he is known) was managing director of the company trading as Manor Farm chickens. His major problem at that time was the quality of feed his growers were receiving from feed mills in the north-east. Calf nuts, pig pencils and turkey pellets were finding their way into chicken feed. The reason why this was such a problem has to do with the critical nature of various trace elements, minerals and vitamins in chicken feed that are very small as a proportion of the total but are critical to performance. He looked into building his own feed mill.

Immediately he encountered three major problems. The bank refused to finance the project on the grounds that Cartons were in the chicken business and not in the feed business. Cavan County Council would not consider granting a licence for a feed mill on the basis that there were plenty of existing mills, and the new feed mill would require a high voltage electricity source, certainly well above that available in the Shercock, Co. Cavan area, and it would have been prohibitively expensive to bring it there.

T.P. is a religious man and when he heard that his sister-in-law believed she'd received favours because of her devotion to a saint named Maximilian Kolbe, he decided he should pray to the same man.

Maximilian Kolbe was a Polish priest who was sent to Auschwitz concentration camp by the Nazis. Escape attempts were punished severely. As a punishment for one such attempt they selected a group of about ten people, one of whom was known to Maximilian as a married man with a family. Maximilian offered to take the place of this man and the Germans accepted. Through prayer and singing hymns, the group survived far longer than normal but after two weeks Maximilian was the last still alive. The Germans finished him off with a lethal injection.

You're not going to believe it, but within a few weeks of T.P. starting his devotion to Blessed Maximilian Kolbe, three amazing things happened. First of all, the bank contacted him to say they had changed their minds and were now interested in financing the project. Secondly, the same Cavan County Council official who'd refused his licence application contacted T.P. to ask if the the new mill would sell its feed to farmers generally. 'No,' was the answer. Its feed was for Manor Farm chickens only.

'OK,' the official said, 'on that basis the licence can be granted.'

And then the ESB announced they were going to build a major power line between Dundalk and the west, which passed close to the proposed site. The new feed mill now had power.

T.P. was convinced that divine intervention took place, so much so that the feed, when produced, was sold under the 'Kolbe' trade name – as it is to this day. I said Kolbe was a saint, but in fact, at the time, he wasn't. T.P. was so profoundly moved by what had happened, he vowed that should Maximilian Kolbe be canonised he would go to Rome for the ceremony. In 1987 Maximilian Kolbe was canonised a saint by Pope John Paul II and T.P. was there. So too was the man whose place the saint had taken in Auschwitz.

I love the stories surrounding my business. I love showing people around the plant. I just love chicken, period. Believe it or not, my father didn't like the taste of chicken and for that reason we didn't get it at home, which is probably why I love it now. I honestly believe food should be good for people and if you think about chicken, there's an awful lot going for it. It's good value, it's low cost but it's low in fat, which is really important in today's world. And it's incredibly versatile. A mother who has twenty minutes from the time she comes in after a full day's work to get a nutritious meal on the table that's different from yesterday's can't do better than chicken.

You look at every culture right across the world and you'll find chicken is not just part of their cuisine but that every single culture has its own variant on how to prepare it. Every one of them. From the Chinese to the Filipinos and Thais – totally different. You come to Europe – just look at the difference between France and England. Portugal, Italy – every one of those has a totally different way of eating chicken. It is the most versatile food, bar none.

One of the lies that's sometimes told about chicken is that it's full of water. Ours isn't. Up until about the mid 1980s here in Ireland, chickens were cooled by being put into a bath of cold water. Needless to say, not only did it lose temperature but it picked up water. The Irish market since then has gone totally to an air-chilled product. No water.

But that's just one of the market changes. The biggest market change came with the emergence of the main supermarket groups. The supermarkets work perfectly well with our integrated chain because it allows them to plan their business well in advance. Promotions on chicken can happen only because companies like mine can plan weeks in advance and have the birds in the right numbers on the right date. That could not happen with the old ways of doing things.

The multiples certainly demanded lower prices because of their volume – but on the other side they gave us the volume to be able to cut the cost to meet those prices. So there was, dare I say it, the chicken and egg situation. Today, of course, the multiples are a dominant force in the industry – 70 per cent or 80 per cent of the market.

The multiples were growing at the same time we were. The market for chicken back in 1970 was around 250,000 birds a week. By 1980 that figure had doubled. It doubled again by 1992. Since then we've only grown by a quarter – in terms of local production. Today, over half of our industry is supplied by imported product.

Of course, we export, too. The Irish market likes fillets.

For every eight fillets we sell here, we sell one leg, whereas in France, for example, there's more demand for legs than for breast. We had to go and sell our legs in those markets and we were doing well, and then avian influenza reached eastern Europe, where we sell the legs. Demand for chicken collapsed, so for six months we couldn't sell a leg. We put them into the freezer and hoped for the best. But we were really pushing our freezer capacity by the end of it.

I found it hard in the last few years, particularly with avian influenza. I was basically defending all the time, saying, 'Look, chicken is every bit as good today as it was two years ago.'

March 2005 was when we started hearing of this new disease in Thailand, and the people who were keeping the poultry were the ones affected. Then in the summer of that year it was reported that it made a huge leap from southern China to Mongolia and to Russia, just north of Mongolia. I remember about August 2005 we were saying, 'Ah, it'll never cross the Urals and we'll be all right as long as it stays over there.' Then there was a breakout in eastern Turkey and within a day or two in Romania. Three children from the one farming family died.

But we were already in a complicated situation here, because a chef named Richard Corrigan went onto *The Tubridy Show* on 23 August and said some pretty awful things about chicken. Sales fell – and wouldn't recover. It was into October before they had recovered and they immediately took a dip from this Turkish and Romanian case.

Of course, you try to fight against dips in the market. You start doing promotions and giving special offers. That raises the demand for the product in about two or three weeks. We did that, but it was six or seven weeks before we recovered. We got through Christmas and then in the first two weeks in January 2006 Turkey had many more cases of avian flu with more people dying.

Two weeks later there was an outbreak on a French turkey farm in the Rhone valley. And that was devastating. It continued in places like Poland and the Czech Republic and eastern Europe and then out of the blue swans contracted it.

The demand dropped 40 per cent in those countries but the supply was still there. The chickens were still on the farm: a huge glut. There was never a shortage of supply. For the first time we saw Italian chicken in Ireland. I've never seen Italian chicken before or since, but at that time I did.

Richard Corrigan popped up again just after the French case appearing on *The Late Late Show* and again said some awful things. This damaged us. Up to this point I had never had to go on TV to try and defend my product. It was a scary, scary thing to do. I'm glad I did it because of the response I received. I now like to get out there and promote the industry and not be on the defensive. I'll drag anybody to the plant and tell them about our safety systems.

We're enormously strong on quality and traceability, but I would accept totally that we have not created a really strong brand. Research conducted by the food labelling group set up by the Minister for Agriculture shows that the number one consideration among consumers when buying chicken is where the it's from. Price is number five. They want to know where it's from and they're right. And the reason they're right is because every time they listen to a food scare the first thing they ask is where the hell the food is from – and it's usually from outside Ireland.

That's why we need to fight hard to get food labelling that tells the consumer where it's from and when it was killed. If I have a chicken fillet and keep it in a chilled cabinet I can show you from date of slaughter that for fourteen days that product is perfect. Why then do I only put nine days on it? I put nine days on because I know the consumer brings it home, puts in the boot of a car, puts it on the counter at home and maybe the fridge is working properly and maybe it's not. In other words it's going to be temperature-abused. So we give up five days of our shelf life to cater for potential temperature abuse.

Imported chicken, by the time it gets to Ireland, is already on day four, yet at that point it gets a nine day label. Their product looks just as fresh, it has the same sell-by date as my product that's day one – theirs is day four. That's not right. But it's EU law. We have to work within that law, within the regulations that derive from EU and Irish law.

In our factory at any moment are six people from the Department of Agriculture, looking at everything from the water we use to the state of the bird, and half of them are working on the final product – bacterial counts and salmonellas and all that sort of stuff is all checked for. In addition to that, we need an EPA licence so we've got the EPA there and we've got Fisheries because we live on a lake and take from it the eight gallons it takes to process a chicken. We use the water, clean it and then send it back out again. I'm glad to say we've been in the same place for the last thirty-six years and so we maintain our environment as well. So, yeah, we've got a huge amount of regulation and then in addition to that there's the Food Safety Authority and the Department of Health for food labelling.

Now, in every single chicken house we have there are two weighing scales that look like a tin of biscuits. Chickens are perching birds, so they love to hop up on the scales. Every time a bird pops up on the scales, it records its weight and it also records the number of weighings it gets in a day. This weighing scales is connected to a computer. Every night it sends into our factory the weight and the number of weighings – for that chicken house.

If our birds go quiet, the weighing would stop and immediately the computer alerts us. So the fact is that here avian influenza will never leave the chicken house, will never get off the farm and the reason is we will know about it before it does. And we know that if it happened, it could be Armageddon for our family business.

Some people have asked me would we not be better if we were still as diversified as we were before Justin and I focused the business. In theory, yes. But I don't think that world exists anymore: a world where you could be in sixteen different businesses in a small way and keep them all going. Just doesn't stand up anymore. Consultants will tell you that you should stick to where you've got a comparative advantage. You can't be a master of everything. We believe we're delivering the best chicken in Ireland and that's where we're going to make our future. Yes, there are threats out there – just as there are everywhere else.

Eleven years ago we set up a six-person R&D team, driven

by the fact that chicken in Ireland is the most consumed meat, largely because we show them more ways to eat chicken. Over the last eleven years we have, every three months, in all of the accounts that we service, brought up a new range of products – new flavours, new presentations, new ways of doing things so that people time and time again when they go to the store will find something new in chicken.

It's an unusual type of R&D. It's hugely successful, despite the fact that only one product has survived over the last eleven years, and that only exists during barbecue time – it's a lovely skewer of inner fillet in a particular sauce and it's a magic product. But outside of that all we're doing is adding new ways of eating chicken all of the time and we've done research on this – what people do is they buy and like the new product but what they'll do is they'll buy the fillet separately next week and they'll make their own sauce. They mix a bit of Uncle Ben's or a bit of curry powder or get a bit of Mr Swartz and mix it with something else and they make their own version of the same idea. So those new product ideas are driving the sale of our basic fillet products.

I'd like to think that we've got better as other processors went out of business. Customers make the final decision as to who they work with. If you ask me are there going to be eight more generations of Cartons in our business, I have to say I doubt it. The likelihood is that one of the continental operators will buy us out and it will make sense because of the economies of scale.

I don't want to think about that, though.

From Part-Time Hobby to Building a National Brand:

The Making of Celtic Bookmakers

Ivan Yates, Celtic Bookmakers

From about eight years of age I was interested in betting. I can remember my first bet. It taught me a great lesson.

My brother, John, at Portora boarding school, would sneak off to the betting shop with his pals. They would put sixpence each way on a horse. Tuppence if the money was a bit tight. I thought this was tremendous. There was no *Racing Post* at the time, just the old *Irish Independent* and it carried a minimum of information. But I was pretty sure I knew how to read form, so while on holidays at home I eyed up my first bet and I decided, 'This one is going to win and that one is going to be second.'

So I had a shilling to win on one and 6d each way on the other. Sure enough, the horse won that I said would win and the other one came in second – and I got less money back than I gave in, because the odds were so short on the winner, and the odds on the each way part on the second one didn't fully cover the cost of the bet. That taught me a lesson. Each time I had a losing bet, I would learn more. I was educating myself in the business I was later going to run.

But basically I loved to go racing. I had an ambition to see every course in Ireland and in the UK. I kept at it, too. At this stage, I've done all the ones in Ireland at least once. In the UK I've only two to go.

I always knew I'd somehow get into the bookmaking business. I remember being in a dormitory in the boarding school, looking out a window and asking myself what I wanted to do with my life.

'I definitely want to get married,' I said. 'I definitely want to have kids. I'd like two boys and two girls. I'm going to live in Blackstoops. I'm going to inherit the family farm there. But I'd really love to be a bookie. I'd really love to be a bookie. And then I'd really love to be Taoiseach as well. I'd love to be in politics as well as farming and bookmaking. Yeah, there's lots of things to be done ...'

I was about eleven or twelve and I was already absolutely focused. Life was not a dress rehearsal. If I wanted these things – and I definitely wanted them – I would have to go for them.

Taking over the farm happened a lot sooner than I was banking on. When I was fourteen, my father, who'd been a forty-a-day smoker all his life, developed lung cancer. He asked me to come home from school and take over the farm. He hadn't worked the farm himself – he'd had it managed for him, because he was a wool merchant, buying and distributing wool all over Ireland, sending it to Britain and further afield.

Now that he was sick, he sold off the wool business and I got ready to take over the farm.

By my mid-teens I was finished with school. I've always been grateful for that. I think I was very fortunate. If you look at the Rich List – the list of rich people in this country – you might be surprised at the number of them who left school early. Yes, they may have gone back to college at night, but leaving school early is probably what turned them into achievers. They realised – as I did – that an early school leaver has to work twice as hard to make up for lack of formal education.

I know I've got to learn every day. What gets me out of bed every morning is that today I will learn something new. I have a huge appetite for learning about any area I don't know about: How does it work? How do you learn to do it? Who's the competition? Who are the mentors?

I did get to spend a year in Gurteen Agricultural College, where I wrote off a tractor and had a great time discovering drink, cigarettes and women, but my father died when I was seventeen, and from then on, the farm was my responsibility. It never struck me, though, that running the farm would necessarily stop me doing the other things I'd decided – when I was all of eleven – that I was going to do. Like politics.

My father had never been keen on me getting involved in politics, not because he was Fianna Fáil, although not active in that party, but because he'd seen other farmers get sucked into the political machine and start neglecting their farm and their family and he was afraid the same would happen to me. His lack of enthusiasm didn't stop me, though. Nothing would have stopped me. Because the period when I was sixteen or seventeen, spending my nights running around the fields in the dark with a flashlight looking for sheep that were having trouble lambing, was precisely the time when Dr Garret FitzGerald had taken the reins in Fine Gael and infused the party with a new openness, a new excitement. How could I not be involved in that?

I'd do my day's farming and head off to a political meeting. You mightn't think of political meetings as social events, but for me they were precisely that. They freed me to do things (like smoking) that I didn't like doing in front of my parents. They involved arguments about tax (I didn't mind paying tax as long as I didn't have to pay too much tax, and at that time everybody was paying too much tax), about the north, about the future. They led to a few pints at the end of the work. Politics, in the beginning, was a great hobby for me.

Of course, if you attend meetings and contribute to them regularly, someone decides you'd be a good district organiser. So I got handed that job. Someone else figures you'd be OK as branch secretary or chairman of Young Fine Gael. With a little more endeavour people want to put you forward for nomination as a candidate for the party ...

All of which meant that before I was out of my teens, I was on the way to two of my dreams: farming and politics. But the marriage thing was well advanced, too.

When I came back from Gurteen, I was going to dances in rural areas, in parish halls. Me and a friend from Gurteen, Rusty, went one night to Bunclody and I saw this cracker of a sixteen-year-old. She was dark and she was a very sexy thing.

'Jesus,' I said to myself, 'I'd love a piece of that now.'

I went over and she brushed me off like dandruff. So I set out to find out all about her. If I want something I really, really go for it. God help her. She had no chance. From about 1978–79 I chased her incessantly. Met her at parties, met her at dances. She would maybe give me a couple of dances and then the brush-off treatment. If I saw her drinking with friends, I'd say, 'Do you want to have a drink?' She'd take a drink all right and I'd say, 'Would you like me to bring you home?'

'No.' Always no.

She'd tell me how she'd be going out with this guy.

'I think he plays under-18 rugby for Ireland,' she'd say vaguely. 'I think he's a winger or something like that.'

'Well, I'm not a complete loser either!' I'd respond.

That went on for a few years. Then, one night, soon after I was elected a TD, I asked, 'Where are you going later on?' and like a flash she said, 'I'll take a lift home from you.'

I was driving my old granny's battered-up Escort at the time. I'll never forget it. It was battered because my granny was a bit of a bumper rider. She had a lot of accidents, little prangs here and there. On the way home from the dance, I pulled in at a lay-by to do a bit of courting and she said, 'How does the seat go back?'

'Just pull the lever,' I said.

I thought she meant slide back. She actually meant recline. The Escort just didn't have that capacity. 'I don't know what you're used to,' I said. 'This car has never reclined!'

That was on a Sunday night. And I said, 'I'll drop up the next Wednesday night. I'll be coming down from the Dáil.'

I was thinking we'd go out for a drink in Tinahealy or

somewhere like that because she lived up in south Wicklow. When I arrived in the Escort (with the non-reclining seats) who came out only the mother-in-law? Kind of with the elbows out and the back arched. She was convinced, when she heard that Deirdre was sort of half going out with a TD, that he had to be married. She came out to take my credentials.

I married Deirdre on the shortest day of the year, the only time I could fit it in, in December 1985. I had built this new bungalow so we could move in after our honeymoon. All the furnishings were in: carpet, beds – nothing too fancy, but a nice dinner table and all that type of thing. The bungalow had dormer windows. The morning of the wedding, heavy rain came and when I arrived to have a pre-wedding bath, I discovered the whole place covered in water. Was I ballistic with the builder. The place was destroyed. But I pulled myself together, went up and got married.

Deirdre was like an antichrist, because the minister, when he got to the 'Do you, Ivan, and do you, Deirdre?' bit, called her Gillian, her sister's name. That drove her mad for starters. In advance, she'd made it clear the whole business of her promising to 'honour and obey' had to be taken out. Made no difference to me. I was easy with it. But we'd no time for a dress rehearsal to iron out the wrinkles, and didn't he leave in honour and obey. We're holding hands at the altar, and Deirdre's nails went right into my finger and I was in agony.

The next day, there were two pictures on the front of the *Sunday Tribune*, one of Deirdre and me, and one of Dessie O'Malley – because we got married on the very day the PDs were founded: 21 December 1985.

We had a great honeymoon in Cyprus. I'd picked the date very carefully so I wasn't missed over Christmas and the New Year, the political process effectively being closed down for that period. I got married to suit my work environment. Deirdre wouldn't have been surprised by that. When she agreed to marry me, I'd jested with her about two things: (a) fasten your seatbelt and (b) I don't carry passengers – you have to pay your way. Deirdre did more than pay her way. She was pivotal to the survival and success of Celtic Bookmakers.

I'm very demanding, as you can see. I'm very driven. The same traits that are useful to me today, in business, when my company, Celtic Bookmakers, is on the cusp of running seventy shops between Ireland and Britain, were essential to me in politics. I have an obsession with punctuality and delivery. If I tell you I'll meet you at one, I'll be there at one. If I tell you I'd complete a task by Thursday, you can expect it on Thursday. I don't believe in sleep or holidays or short breaks. I can't bear the current trend for young people to go to university, do one degree, then do a masters, then do a doctorate, and in their late twenties decide that now they need to see the world.

By the time they get launched on their working life, ten years have been wasted. And then they're resentful when they've difficulty getting a mortgage?

One of the great mistakes I believe companies make when recruiting is looking at the academic achievements on the CV, which tell you nothing about how the person's going to perform in real life. In real life, what makes for success is hard work and persistence. Not qualifications. Not letters after your name.

Because I had energy, I ended up on the ticket for an urban council seat when I was still a teenager. My campaign covered more ground with more energy than had been seen in years, while making every possible mistake. I made all the mistakes newcomers make and then some. Mistakes are no problem, the first time. Everybody needs to make them as part of learning. Making the same mistake twice is the mark of a loser. I've made many mistakes, but rarely the same one twice.

There was a great urgency to the learning, because that campaign was in 1977 and a general election was coming up fast. I was approached to run. At the time, I didn't even have a car. I did have a provisional driver's licence, so that was the time I went around to where my grandmother used to live before she went into a nursing home, and hauled out her Ford Escort. It was old. It was dented. It was eaten up with rust. Its seats (as Deirdre discovered) couldn't recline.

But I got it running, and that was my vehicle for the campaign. I probably covered more ground in it in a couple of months than it had covered in all its years up to that point. I never stopped. Except for the couple of days I was laid up in bed due to asthma, exacerbated by smoking. And I was the second candidate elected in my constituency. Eventually, I was Minister for Agriculture in John Bruton's coalition government with the Labour Party.

While farming and doing politics, I kept up the interest in betting. I'd make mistakes and beat myself up about them. I'd be like a raging bull for six weeks if I lost a lot of money.

But it wasn't just about betting. It was about the places where betting happened. It was about the characters who were bookmakers at the time. Like Pat Boland, who I met in his betting shop in the west. The owner, one of the real old-style independent bookies. The kind that'd take the lining out of your pockets and not keep the shop that clean. He had a great saying: 'Where there's a little take a lot, where there's a lot, take it all.'

He would watch me. Watch my pattern of betting. At the time, for instance, Henry Cecil was a very popular trainer. He still is. But he'd have a lot of very short-price horses. I'd see a 1/3 shot and I'd lay £1,000 to win. I'd only have the one bet for the day.

'Would you be interested in this game?' he asked me one day.

I said I would.

'It's the greatest game,' he told me. 'Thirty per cent profit. You take in £900, you keep £300. You take in £3,000 a week in bets, you keep £1,000 of that. You give £300 for your staff, £300 for your rent, hold on to the rest and you've £300 a week for yourself. It beats working. I don't know what you're wasting your time with that politics for.'

There is a leap of faith before committing to starting any new business. There is the risk, uncertainty, fear of failure and potential financial loss ... The moment I felt compelled to open our first betting shop was when I read the Mark McCormack book, *What they don't teach you at Harvard Business School.* In the final chapter he asks how do you know whether you are suited to be an entrepreneur. He says that it's not that you'd be great at sales or profits – rather that you would never forgive yourself on your deathbed if you hadn't tried it.

I decided I'd go for it and open a bookmaker's shop. I wouldn't open one in Wexford, a) because I didn't want people to think I was losing my political focus, which I wasn't, and b) if it was a total tits-up disaster, I needed it to be somewhere removed from me and not noticeable. I picked Tramore and opened on St Stephen's Day, 1987.

I will never forget that first day's trading. I was a complete greenhorn. We were run off our feet. I came home late that night with literally bundles of cash. I thought this was the best thing ever. I was addicted to bookmaking. Little did I know what horrors lay ahead.

We were expecting our first baby. Andrew was born in January 1988. It was peculiar corporate planning, but each time we'd have a new baby, we'd open a new office at the same time. It was one a year for a while. Of each.

Tramore taught me my first location lesson, which was never to go for a short-term lease, because you've no equity in the building. The shop was too small and because of the short lease, it made no sense to do it up. The second location was Wicklow town.

While I was determined to expand, to create a chain, the betting tax was crippling. You'd put a £100 on a horse and you'd have to pay £10 on top of that in tax. The punter had to pay the tax and they didn't like it. So as soon as I showed signs of ambition, Paddy Power went tax free just to put me out of business. I was only a minnow in the business, but they decided to announce that all bets with them were tax free. They would subsidise the punter, at whatever cost was entailed. I had to do likewise.

It was very painful, I had to subsidise the losses out of my Dáil salary. This was in 1988. It was actually costing me £400 or £500 a month to keep the business going. An absolute nightmare. Deirdre was still teaching. I borrowed money from my mother and I was glad it was a once-off loan because although I'm not much more than a nominal Protestant, going to church at Christmas and Easter at a push, my mother's father and grandfather were all prominent clergymen who would have choked before they would have accepted that their grandson would have been a bookie.

Every time I got ready to pay her back, I ended up borrowing more money from her. It wasn't just Paddy Power taking such savage action against the newcomer. I hadn't a clue about proper controls and systems on either side of the counter. I was a lamb to the slaughter of fraud and sharp practice. This had to be sorted out without bringing the business to its knees. The end result is that at one point, my mother – who wasn't at all enthusiastic about bookmaking in the first place – was propping up the business with an £18,000 loan and we were losing about £600 a month. To put that in context: my Dáil salary at the time was maybe £1,000 a month.

That was where Deirdre came in. Without her, Celtic Bookmakers would have folded. She became the licensed bookmaker, sole trader and lease holder, took over the payroll early on and became company secretary. She was never interested in gambling but she was a much better judge of character than me. To this day, she is still in charge of personnel and security. Celtic Bookmakers became a limited company, with

99 per cent of the shares in the name of Deirdre Boyd. I gave my old friend Pat Boland the other 1 per cent share. Deirdre gave up teaching because we now had three kids and she couldn't do everything.

One of the people in business I totally admire is Michael O'Leary. He had one simple philosophy: high volume, low margin. Pile 'em high, sell 'em cheap. In bookmaking this meant giving the punter/consumer the best value.

My philosophy was to give the best odds. Full stop. No matter what Paddy Power or Ladbrokes or anyone was doing, I was always going to give the best odds. I put it on our logo and on my business card: No one beats our bonuses. In any town in Ireland or the UK or anywhere else, underneath our logo, is that slogan. No one beats our bonuses. We match and better what everyone else does.

Here's an example. There are around 10,000 betting shops in the UK; 1,170 betting shops in Ireland. Let's say it's late afternoon and there's a 5.30 race this evening at Leicester. Ten minutes before the 5.30 race they beam in live pictures and data on the prices from the guys on the course writing up the odds. So they're the same in every betting shop.

I figured out a way to tackle that, a way to make Celtic Bookmakers uniquely different. It works this way. You come in and say, 'I got a tip for Number 1 in the 5.30.' You put a tenner on at 2/1 and to your horror it went out on price to 4/1 – everyone else heard about the same horse. But if it came in, you'd normally only get 2/1. I decided to change that.

'If it goes out to 4/1,' I said, 'I'll pay you at 4/1. So you're in a no-lose situation. If it goes in you're at the right price and if it goes out you're at the best price.'

That cost Celtic Bookmakers 1.7 per cent but it meant my competitors had two choices. They could watch their turnover walk out their door and in my door because I gave better value or they could match my odds, and my overheads were lower than theirs so either way I won. It was a 'Gotcha'. Simple as that.

'We try to focus on three key things in Celtic Bookmakers,' I tell new staff on first meeting. 'We give the best value. Our gross profit margins are 3 per cent below our competitors'. Secondly, we spend millions every year in doing up our shops: we have air conditioning, we have free tea, coffee, soup. We have nice facilities, we have modern screen systems, we have plush seating, proper flooring in very spacious modern shops. The third thing we do – and the most important – is give great customer service.'

Now, everyone from Bank of Ireland to Guinness to Fianna Fáil say they do great customer service. It's such a clichéd hackneyed load of bullshit. This is what I mean by customer service in Celtic Bookmakers' terms. The Lotto is on every Wednesday and Saturday. Six balls are pulled out and a seventh ball is called the bonus ball. We put out a sheet, numbered 1–45. If Michael Gaffney comes in, he doesn't even have to lay a bet, just put his name against number 3 or number 33. If the bonus ball on the three draws comes out with his number he gets a free bet. We invest over €200K a year in this. What's the key point? Not the cost of the free bets. The key point is that now I know your name is Mike Gaffney. The next day he comes in I say, 'How are you today, Mike.' Mike is treated as an individual, a human. Our own people have name badges, so he gets to know Mary or Bob and there's a little bit of banter: Man U are going well, Tiger is going bad. Shamrock Rovers, Tipperary hurlers ...

Our people have to have the same skills a barman has. Punters are temperamental. You need to leave them alone one day, have a chat with them the next. The atmosphere in a shop has to be welcoming but not invasive. Which in turn means the setting has to be right. When I look for location, I want 1,200 sq ft (22 ft x 50/60 ft – a perfect box). Size matters. Each customer must have their own space. I'm a tough negotiator. I don't pay VAT, the landlord must deal with that. He must provide customer toilets and air conditioning ducts. I have a set pro forma approach, based on learning from earlier mistakes: standard lease, five-year rent reviews, always long-term leases.

A handy tip I learned many years ago from a smart auctioneer was to shut your mouth. At the key point of negotiation, once you have made your best offer, reached your walk away point – you just stop talking. The human instinct is always to fill the void of silence. This usually means a concession by the other side.

What I look for are three vital factors: Pubs. Not yuppy-boy-meets-girl cocktail bars. I mean the kind of pub that's got pictures of Istabraq, the hurling team and Dawn Run on the wall. The TV playing the racing channel. I need parking. It has to be convenient for customers at, say, lunchtime, to nip in, nip out preferably without being seen: so dual front and back entrance. (The bank manager doesn't want to be seen going in and out of the betting shop.) Pubs, parking and pedestrian traffic (footfall) are all important. Tertiary locations don't work.

What I try and do, be it in Swansea or anywhere else, is not have a shop at every crossroads but have a magnet in the centre of Swansea so that people from all over will come in off the bus, off the train. When she goes shopping, he'll go punting. When he goes drinking, he's beside where he can enjoy his drink and watch his Channel 4 racing.

Above all, I provide value. Customers will go that extra mile for the value. In every race, we have tweaked systematically, like Ryanair have done, the terms in favour of the customer. It's simple. Not like making you book on the internet thirty days in advance with a deposit and you must be wearing four red shoes. In every race, every day we give better value.

The *Racing Post* is the bible. They provide everybody's prices. Let's say there's a football match on today. In the *Racing Post*, the bold black print gives the best price. So we guarantee the black print. On every first and last goalscorer. Half time–full time double results. All dead heats in dog and horse races are paid to the full stake on both winners. We systematically give the best value.

Because we're not one of the giants – although we're making progress – we have to run harder to stand still. But we're driven, too, because of being Irish and being a family business.

For a while I was doing politics and bookmaking at the same time. Something Roddy Doyle once said, about being a teacher before he was a writer, applies to my political career.

He said something like: 'For nine years I loved teaching. For three years it was a good salary. For the last two years I hated it.'

That's exactly the way I felt about politics. I loved it for about eighteen years – up to 1997. I didn't entirely love being a minister; I found it very pressurised. I took it very seriously. I found it stressful. BSE and the EU presidency and flying and being told to go here and there and being told to do eighteen things a day. I wasn't in charge. I was nominally in charge but I wasn't really in charge. I was a bigger doormat than I was as a TD. However, there was both a great buzz and huge job satisfaction in being a minister. You could get things done and make things happen. Being in government, at the cabinet table, running a department is as good as it gets in politics.

The reasons I left politics? In no particular order …

Repetition. Monotony. I was burnt out from the constituency work – I physically hated having to go to branch meetings about the same pothole. It was doing my head in. It was gone past boredom, it was actually annoying me and every autumn it was coming around again. I liked the people, I could have a drink with them, enjoy their company … it was just having to have to do the same routine and the deadly predictable format. The endless ritual began to get to me.

The same for clinics. I got great satisfaction out of helping people. But when you're doing the seventeenth thing for the same person, it begins to feel pointless. I didn't go into politics to be a social and community worker, and increasingly the competitive pressure on politicians was to be that. What the public want, the public should get. If that's what you've got to do, don't bitch about it, just do it. I began to realise that if I wasn't prepared to do it, I should get out.

When I went into politics, I was a young fella, I'd go out for a smoke and a drink and meet the lads and it was all bright-eyed, bushy-tailed, starry-eyed and new. But now, after twenty years of being a TD, I was over forty, I had four kids. Even when I was home, my mind was miles away. I was out every night of the week.

When the bi-centenary of 1798 came up, for example, I was at every crossroads each Sunday watching pike men, instead of being at home. I was missing out on family life and I realised my kids were missing out. I was a bad father and not a very good husband. I wasn't impressed with that. Like all youngsters, when I was twenty I was sure I was going to die at forty. Fortunately, I'd given up the fags on 6 August 1997. Had my last cigarette at a quarter past six that evening.

Financially, I realised that I was missing out on the potential of the bookmaking business. Paddy Power was launched the same year as I opened my first shop, but now they had eighty shops while I had only nine. There is no capital appreciation in politics. In fact it's just the opposite. In addition, I was at the maximum point in the pension scale. If I was in the Dáil for forty more years, I'd still get the same pension.

Many ministers loved being ministers. I didn't feel that way about it – it was just a tough but great job. However, the adrenaline of being minister was now being replaced by the drudgery of opposition. The inane and tiresome requisite to politically maul ministers as opposition spokesperson lost its novelty and appeal. I had come to reject any bullshit notion

GALWAY COUNTY LIBRARIES

of legacy, of being remembered for something. When you're a minister, even if you're a good minister, you're like a 26A bus; there's another one coming along. There's another minister coming along.

I wasn't going to allow my career or my life to be decided at the ebb and flow of the last political atrocity. It was my career to implode, to self destruct, to end, to do what I liked with. But also I felt deep down something an auld cattle dealer once said to my wife: 'The Yates',' he said, 'they'd be more fond of the pound than the power. They'd be reared that way.'

I thought afterwards how true it was.

At the end of the day, I cannot deny I am a total opportunist. I feared the prospects of Fine Gael returning to government in 2002 were remote. Whereas I felt that in business I had a great opportunity. I could build a national brand. That's my goal for Celtic Bookmakers. Whether it has eighty shops or 120 shops, whether it has €300m turnover or twice that, my goal is to build an indestructible business, whether it's family owned or not.

Celtic Bookmakers has gone through a number of stages. First was learning how to run a functioning betting shop. Organic growth and one-off acquisitions built this up to a dozen shops. We converted from sole trader status to incorporation. Every penny of profit and cash flow went into expansion. Having learned from our mistakes and gotten six inches off the ground, it became easier to move up to thirty shops. At that stage, banks want to lend to you, landlords want you as their tenant and good staff apply for jobs.

A legendary Irish bookmaker is supposed to have said,

'You are not a real bookmaker until you have gone bust three times.' I can recall three separate periods when I could not sleep properly at night with the fear that Celtic Bookmakers might not survive.

The first time was when I had to borrow the eighteen grand from my mother. I also came close to losing all when trying to diversify into on-course betting and developing phone clients. At that time Istabraq was winning his three champion hurdles. His first one cost me £100,000 I did not have. Then, 2005 was annus horribilis – every favourite seemed to win, and a tax discount war between bookies broke out. Put simply, we were paying the 2 per cent betting tax for the punter, but our net target profit was 1 per cent. This meant a minus 1 per cent net situation.

At the same time, the British Horse Racing Board (BHB) put a data levy on us for their racing information. All in all, we lost about a million quid. I couldn't expand any more out of cash flow. All the plcs were issuing profit warnings. It wasn't just me, other bookmakers were also in desperate straits.

I really needed the results in Christmas 2005 to break right for me. They didn't. We had our worst ever Christmas and lost another quarter of a million. We'd be having family parties and the in-laws and the outlaws would all be coming and I would be doing my nut. I'll never forget New Year's Eve, 2005. We had our blackest day ever. We lost another €80,000.

Then the tide began to turn. First, the betting tax was reduced to 1 per cent. Second, we won a high court case against the BHB. Instead of having to pay an £18 million bill, we didn't have to pay anything. That brought me back into profit and made me decide to go on the borrowing trail to get eighty shops developed.

In the modern business environment, the toughest battle is for the independents to survive against the omnipotent plcs. In every high street and business sector, from video rentals, fashion, coffee shops, electrical goods, airlines, hotels, travel agents, insurance, manufacturing, drinks – plcs have deeper pockets, more muscle and ruthless management. If they can't beat you down they'll try and buy you out.

To survive and grow I've had to restructure the business. Instead of trying to do everything yourself, you must hire the best people. In the last year, I've recruited a financial controller, race room manager, HR manager. Whereas I used to take all the bets, now I have it all delegated to a proper professional studio in Enniscorthy. I have two operations managers hired from Ladbrokes and William Hill. My goal is to build a team that can compete and win.

Last year we bought Joe Molloy's. This year we have just acquired UBET. The racing studio is to enable Celtic Book-makers tele betting. Twenty per cent of all bets now are over the phone. So we've moved into that market and built it up to almost 2,000 customers in a short period of time. We're going to build that into a €20 million business.

Our target is to have seventy-five to eighty shops in two years' time, and, by the end of 2009 to be taking in €230 million a year between here and the UK, with a telephone business doing €20 million a year. That will throw off enough income to put into a schedule of debt repayment and give me a national brand that's indestructible.

Then I will sit down and think about the next phase. I've had various offers: management buy-in, equity-share investment proposals and acquisition bids. It's probably inevitable to go the dot com route. My goal is to keep as many of the shares for as long as I can and to build the brand as big as I can.

So it's very much work in progress and we're on a solid development plan. Last year, we did €150 million and made €2 million profit. It's going well. Results in 2007 were brilliant for the bookies. They were crap in 2005, great in 2007.

Many of my political friends cannot understand why I gave up politics. I believe the energy you get from following your passion is remarkable. Twice, I have made my hobby my livelihood. I went to political meetings because I loved politics – I couldn't get enough of it. But after over twenty years I did get enough of it. The excitement, the highs and lows of gambling was my other true passion (not forgetting Deirdre). I get a real buzz out of developing this pastime into a serious business. Despite the 'nosebleeds' of Aidan O'Brien training another big Irish winner in the UK, Ruby Walsh riding a treble, Kerry or Man U winning yet again – I've learned the most important requirement to be a bookie is to have an even temperament to cope with heavy losses.

Every day I try to learn something new. Most of all I try to look forward, avoid regrets and stay hungry …

A Drop of the Craytuir

Richard Barrett, Treasury Holdings

Conventional medical wisdom tells us that limited quantities of red wine help with blood pressure stabilisation, cholesterol reduction and longevity attainment. During the course of my work, I have had to travel extensively in every continent and, in the course of same, I have come to have an ongoing friendship with restaurant wine lists, especially favouring obscure grape varieties, regional specialities and outright spectacular great wines. This acquaintance, also shared by my partner, Johnny Ronan (who has acute taste buds when it comes to willingly mortgaging the company's asset base for a rare vintage at lunchtime – he has a pay by instalment facility at Patrick Guilbauds), stood us in good, but somewhat unexpected, stead on a recent important acquisition.

Battersea Power Station is pivotally located in London near Chelsea Bridge on the south bank of the great sweeping body of water that bisects London, the river Thames, a mere 2,000 metres from the Palace of Westminster (which has a surprisingly poor wine list, but one which doesn't seem to deter the members from giving it a lash in medically unwise quantities). It is the world's largest brick building, formed the backdrop for the cover of the Pink Floyd album, *Animals* (the one where the pink pigs are floating by) and is definitively the greatest remaining undeveloped riverside site in central London, being c.40 acres of the primest real estate imaginable.

If you were ever tempted to buy a site deserving of an afternoon on the Petrus after you had done so, this was it. We had tried to buy the site for almost three years, but had failed to agree terms with the owners (disagreeing on a variety of issues), a wealthy Hong Kong family called Hwang in Cantonese but Wang in their native Taiwanese dialect. We had mouthwateringly come close a couple of times, but could never quite get agreement on 100 per cent ownership or leaving them with the residential portion, etc. The site lay tantalisingly waiting for a saviour, legs akimbo, breasts appetisingly on openish display. We laid in patient wait, hoping for the right moment, which eventually arrived.

I was spending most of my time in China, where Treasury was establishing large-scale real estate operations in Shanghai, Qindao and Beijing. China represents a gigantic opportunity on a scale never seen before, and we decided to grab that chance with both hands. I was fortunate that I was accompanied in that task by some of Treasury's finest people, who proved skilful at adapting to Chinese ways in a manner few westerners do. For their talent, dedication, hard work, stamina and iron stomachs, I am enormously grateful, for Chinese dinners are not the occasion of large-scale imbibing of Moutons or Lafites, but the Chinese firewater known as baiju, a grandfather and much more powerful version of our own poitín. For all those long nights gasping under the onslaught of ganbei (sláinte) toasts, we owe our thanks for where we are in China today to Rob, Dave, Rory, Dyfed, Hugh and the more intermittent Guy, Jodie, Niall, Chris and Yvonne.

In September 2006, the waiting hunters were rewarded for their patience. The Hwangs, the only non major oil company to be awarded exploration licences in the South China Sea, struck huge quantities of gas off Wenzhou on one of their blocks (they had been awarded territory roughly the size of Switzerland). This necessitated the unwavering attention of Victor Hwang and also his physical presence in China, much more than in London, where he had spent the previous ten years. Having kept in regular contact with the Hwangs, we pounced. I went to see Victor and we established a rough formula, under which they would be prepared to sell the site to us.

China is a different place to Europe, full of ancient traditions, customs opposite to our own and a way of doing business based on the personal relationship between two parties, rather than contracts. I had learned that way of doing business in the Hot Pot restaurants of China's major cities, of spectacularly lavish private dining-rooms in the most splendid of settings near the Forbidden City where relationships were formed, strengthened and enhanced over bird's nest soup, sharks' fins, braised python, the slug-like sea cucumber and the aphrodisiac jellyfish, all washed down with copious quantities of baiju. That arduous training came in useful.

There then followed a series of dinners in Hong Kong and Shanghai, where the flesh of the deal was put on its bones,

but not before the Hwangs sought to figure me out. No deal
is ever done in China without the parties engaging in an
elaborate choreographed sequence of a type of mating dance,
where, over dinner, they figure out if are you the sort of chap
they'd do business with. Woe betide the westerner who tries
to cut the dating process short or doesn't keep up his end by
lashing back equal quantities to them as they judge you when
you're in your cups.

Victor Hwang is an artistic type, bubbling full of ideas that
fall helter skelter from his active brain. But the 'father' of the
family is George, the eldest of the four brothers, an enjoyable
character who is a bit of a rascal but who has one of Asia's
finest private wine collections and, without doubt, one of the
three best cigar collections in the world. He has two full-time
wine sommeliers and also one for the cigars (despite speaking
Spanish, I don't know the Havana equivalent of sommelier).

George decided to grill me and provided one of the most
difficult oenological tests ever set. And then he discovered, in
a chance remark I made about a dusty Sassicaia, that I knew
a thing or two about wine, garnered from all those Malbecs
and Syrahs and Grenaches and Cabernets and Tempranillos
and Merlots that I had spent years around the globe slurping,
never thinking it would come in useful in such an arduous
examination. It's difficult to describe George's great joy when
he found someone that enjoyed the pleasures of the grape as
much as himself. And when he did, the wine flowed and the
vintages kept coming one after another after another. To give
a flavour of the negotiations, I set down hereunder two of the
menus I 'underwent' with the Hwangs:

Dinner 1

(10 courses, 7 hours)

Montrachet 1999
Ch Lafite 1989
Ch La Tour 1982
Ch Petrus 1986 (Magnum)
Grange 1986
Corton 1911
Cohiba 1492 (only 300 boxes ever made)
Cohiba Double Robusto
Davidoff Dom Perignon

Dinner 2

(8 courses, 6 hours)

Meursault Domaine Lafon 1992
Ch Cheval Blanc 1975 (Magnum)
Ch Lafite 1989
Ch Mouton Rothschild 1989
Ch Haut Brion 1990
Ch Clinet 1989
Ch Legay 1989
1891 Havanas from a sunken galleon
1992 Churchills

I am thrilled we bought Battersea, but I'll never forget the way it was bought, the negotiations in London, Dublin, Shanghai and Hong Kong, the ups and downs of the deal, the volatile participants and, most especially, the extraordinary way we did it, drowning ourselves in some of the world's best wines, supplied by as generous a heart as you'd ever find.

Just shows, you can't beat a drop of the craytuir.

Fast Food and a Competitive Attitude

Brian Ranalow, H&K

Irish people, starting from a small factory in Ballyfermot, rising through the ranks of a multinational to end up running the entire group and eventually owning it. That's our story.

Today H&K is headquartered in Dublin, employs nearly a thousand people worldwide and is a leading global supplier of complete restaurant kitchen systems to the major chains, particularly fast food chains such as McDonald's – our biggest customer.

The H&K story really starts not in Ireland but in Canada in 1975, when a plumbing contractor named Bill Griffiths was doing some work for the McDonald's restaurants in Toronto. One of the McDonald's senior management invited him to have a look at a company called H&K, standing for 'hospital and kitchen equipment', which was in trouble.

Bill was a tremendous salesman with a very strong personality and he was highly respected by the McDonald's people. He bought H&K for 50c on the dollar and brought in his son, his accountant and lawyer as shareholders. Three years later, in 1978, McDonald's were looking to expand in Europe at a time when a McDonald's restaurant was something of a rarity over here. Importing their kitchen equipment from the United States wasn't an attractive prospect. So Bill Griffiths was offered an opportunity.

'Well, would you like to set up something for us in Europe?'

A couple of his people went to London and looked around. Then the IDA heard about it and went into overdrive, bringing them across to Dublin and offering the usual support if they set up in Ireland. They also found them a potential partner in the form of Avenue Investments, the family empire created by the late Joe McGrath, founder of the Irish Sweepstakes and Waterford Glass. So a small factory was established in Ballyfermot, employing around fifty people and fabricating stainless steel complete kitchen packages for McDonald's in Europe.

In the mid 1980s, I was an engineer in my thirties looking for a new challenge and noticed this very attractive ad in *The Irish Times* offering a big salary for those times. Seán McHale, the well-known rugby player, handled the recruitment, and after several interviews with the H&K people I got the job, started work in the factory in Ballyfermot – and experienced something of a shock. The company was not in the state that had been presented to me at the interviews. Productivity was a disaster. Quality was poor. The relationship with the customer was very difficult. Management capability was weak. Virtually everything had to be fixed. It turned out that I was one of a series of managing directors in the short history of H&K in

Europe – my immediate predecessor had departed suddenly following what sounded like a nervous breakdown!

In my first year there, we only produced about fifteen or twenty kitchen packages in the whole year. Each one took an incredible number of hours to put together. The place was inflexible and the people were under-motivated and highly unionised. The only principle was that deliveries had to be met. If that meant flying in equipment from Canada to meet customer deadlines, equipment was flown in from Canada. That happened – despite the fact that the production team on the factory floor were all working through the night to the absolute last minute. Which meant that people worked incredible overtime, which made no corporate sense, but made great sense to the workers, because they had a deal whereby if they worked through the night they got double or treble over-time. Those payments were referred to as 'ghosters'.

It was a complete mess, but I was not as dispirited as I might have been, partly because I could always see potential in it. The sister companies in the United States and Canada were doing well and it was clear that H&K Europe was a business which, if it was fixed, could be developed into something internationally powerful. If you were in a business in Ireland in the late 1970s and early 1980s, the challenge was to find orders. I was in an oddly more positive position. The orders were there – all we had to do was find a way of putting them together. It would be tough going but I could not say I ever had any feelings that it was not going to work out.

After a few months in the job, it became obvious that there was no way forward in terms of actually managing the labour situation towards an acceptable level of productivity. I was spending most of my time on the factory floor chasing metal through the system and monitoring each delivery as it went down to the wire. With three unions in place, and a very complicated bonus system, every tiny change had to be negotiated, and probably half of my time went on resolving labour issues. We had a demanding customer who had to be satisfied. The UK was the biggest market for us, so the solution, as I saw it, was to set up a separate operation in the UK.

In June 1986 we set up a plant in Rugby in the middle of the UK, which, strategically, was a good location. We planned it down to the last detail. We did everything right. We got the right people on board and if they weren't right, we got rid of them immediately. Because it was a professionally managed operation, it started to succeed very quickly and that in turn put pressure on the Irish plant to start getting its act together.

Unfortunately, although some productivity improvements were achieved, the Irish plant never really got its act together, and had to be closed down at the beginning of the 1990s. By that point, we were manufacturing in Mexico as well as in Rugby. It was a tough decision and it was particularly tough on some hard-working employees who had done their best to make the Dublin operation work.

However, although we ceased production in Ballyfermot, we only mothballed the factory and we kept the Dublin office going, which accommodated the financial, engineering and marketing functions for H&K in Europe – these functions were also in need of a major overhaul. The accounts function, for example, was very weak and we urgently needed good information to feed into all areas of the business. Accordingly, we beefed up the finance area by recruiting newly qualified accountants: professionals coming into a business where there weren't many professionals – this was a metal-bashing business, operated by draughtsmen and sheet metal workers who were elevated to engineering and management functions. In that context the finance function was a logical way to start the massive change required and ensure that professionals were running the business. Pat Healy had been brought in as financial controller in the late 1980s and he did a great job in recruiting young accountants into his department who were then funnelled into other functions to provide professional, systematic management in areas such as inventory control, logistics and even marketing. When Pat Healy retired, David Spain joined as chief financial officer.

By bringing in these young people, we were creating a strong Irish management who were not carrying any baggage from the past, and who could therefore come to terms with the whole international business and eventually buy the whole business and own it themselves. David Bobbett, for example, who is today CEO of the entire H&K group and a significant shareholder, qualified with KPMG and came to us as a temporary accountant in 1986. He later moved into logistics and then sales and became a key player in establishing new standards of performance in H&K Europe. Other key young recruits in the late 1980s/early 1990s were Keith Cassidy, Daniel O'Mahony, Patrick MacCann and Eddie Hudson, who with David Bobbett provided a core of management excellence which drove the whole business forward.

By the early 1990s H&K Europe was no longer the 'poor cousin' in the H&K Group and it was becoming apparent that the Irish management team was out-performing their United States colleagues. In 1991, I was appointed chief operating officer of the group and shortly afterwards CEO as Bill Griffiths moved to chairman. David Bobbett followed a similar path just a few years behind me – he became managing director, Europe, in the mid 1990s, then group COO, and by 2002 was group CEO, as I moved to chairman. David, as an accountant, and I, as an engineer, combined incredibly well in spite of our backgrounds in different disciplines. Perhaps it was on account of these differences that the combination worked so well – David is very analytical and commercially focused, whereas I was more interested in the product and strategic customer issues.

During the 1990s, the United States business was seriously under-performing. We were profitable, but large sales volumes compensated for inefficiencies in the system and a major overhaul was necessary. A succession of presidents for the United States business served for two years apiece without much success until our long-serving marketing VP, Noel Kohler, agreed to take on the job. At that time our headquarters was in Dallas, and North America represented probably 80 per cent of group sales. We had tremendous opportunities in the United States but I resisted the pressure to move to Dallas by committing to travel to the States and spending one week every month there. It was a hard slog over those years, with too many air miles. As well as travel to the United States, Canada and Mexico, we were also opening up new markets. This meant frequent visits to European destinations were necessary and then came the trips to China and Australia. Because of the shortage of competent middle managers in our North American business, we ended up putting in people from Europe to sort out all the systems. They went over there spending months at a time, over a period of two years, installing new systems and more organised management. These Irish managers had a practical, common sense approach to identifying problems and solving them and this approach became fundamental to the H&K culture. With Noel's leadership and the support of the Irish team, together with some important new recruits to the Dallas team, the North American situation started to turn around and is now a key profit centre for the group.

So we have traced how a group of Irish managers, with a professional approach and a capacity for travel and hard work, gradually became the driving force behind the turnaround of an American-based multinational. But what about opportunities for these managers to acquire some equity in the business? By the early 1990s, I showed an interest in ownership by offering to buy out the European business. The offer may not have been taken too seriously but my ambitions were generously supported by the Irish shareholders – at that stage Mercury Asset Management had bought out the 25 per cent holding of Avenue Investments. They knew that if they wanted me to stay on board, which they did, something needed to be done. That's when I got my first shares in the business.

In 1995, Mercury and two of the Canadian shareholders wanted to exit, and by buying out their 50 per cent share the remaining shareholders saw their percentage shareholding double. The process each time was to gear up the business by using bank money and then work down the debt over three or four years. In 1999, Bill Griffiths was ready to retire and cash in his chips and pass on the chairman's job to his son, Gerry. This resulted in 90 per cent of the business being owned by Gerry and me. The remaining ownership was spread among the senior managers and our only non-executive director, Peter Murray. Peter, who was then serving as chairman of Anglo Irish Bank, had a long association with H&K, dating back to the days when he was financial director with Avenue Investments in the 1980s.

In 2002, it was time for Gerry to exit. He held about 66 per cent, and his exit would have a major impact on the remaining shareholders. We now had the opportunity to significantly increase the equity owned by the senior managers, simultaneously reducing my shareholding over a period. However, the first job was to buy Gerry out and we needed serious bank support to achieve that. Our bank for the previous fifteen years was JP Morgan Chase, and they had financed the two previous buyouts without too much hassle. However, at the time JP Morgan Chase were dealing with some fallout from the Enron collapse and, in order to play safe, they decided to set up a syndicate, bringing in two other banks, to provide a loan of €50m. While we thought we had a deal agreed in April, it dragged on month after month and by September they had changed the terms several times. We felt we were being messed around and there was no future with a three-bank syndicate who could not make up their minds.

Peter Murray, being chairman of Anglo Irish Bank,

suggested we talk to his people and within a week they had the deal done. So Anglo became our bankers in 2002 and they have been great partners in the last five years as our business has gone through a period of exciting growth. Last year we did another turn where I further reduced my shareholding from 45 per cent down to 15 per cent. We brought on more managers as shareholders. So now there is a young team of people who essentially own the business and run it and manage it out of Ireland. The last four years represent probably the latest and best chapter in the H&K story, with David Bobbett and his team building on a solid platform to achieve phenomenal improvement in performance.

H&K is now an Irish business, operating globally but headquartered in Dublin. All the financing and all of the risk and major customer relationships are handled and managed out of Ireland. Group purchasing and the financial control are in Dublin and a significant amount of our group business is channelled through Ireland. Having Ireland as a base for running a global logistics business, even if the product doesn't go through Ireland, makes good sense from a business point of view.

Our business is a mix of manufacturing and logistics. The manufactured product is high-quality stainless steel fabrication which has to be very durable for a high-volume restaurant. Typically, if you go into a McDonald's restaurant, we supply and install the complete equipment package you see behind the counter – manufacturing probably a third of it. The logistics business can bring together a complete package of equipment, deliver it to a restaurant site anywhere in the world and have it up and running in a matter of weeks. This capability allows big chains to open restaurants and grow very quickly.

The key part of our business lies in supporting a big restaurant chain to develop and expand. We do this, not just by supplying the equipment package they will need as they open, but also by supporting the restaurants after they have opened. Minimising equipment downtime is critical and we have steadily expanded our spare parts service. Of increasing value is our capacity to remodel restaurants, changing out equipment to meet the needs of menu changes. What is most important is that we go in and do the work overnight and we can change thousands of restaurants in a matter of months to meet the deadline of a new marketing campaign.

Our biggest manufacturing operation is now in Mexico. In Dallas, we also have a big manufacturing operation as well as our main warehousing centre for the United States, where we consolidate packages for delivery out to restaurants. In Canada, we again have a similar kind of warehousing and service operation outside Toronto.

In Rugby we have manufacturing and warehousing which supports all of Europe. We have a significant operation in Australia which we opened in 1999, setting up a warehousing/sales and service operation there. Australia is a very good market for us, particularly with McDonald's and also chains like Subway.

Today we employ just under 1,000 people and while we used to have a number of Irish people at different outposts, this has changed over time so that, these days, in most countries, local management is doing the job. In Australia, for example, a young Irish guy went out there to set it all up. He was out there for two years, then he came home and now it's all run by local people.

In our Dublin headquarters, there is a multinational mix of people on account of all the language skills that are needed, because the European sales operation is also run out of Dublin. You walk through the office and you'll hear a number of different languages supporting the different countries that we're selling into.

H&K has never had a high profile in Ireland, mainly because 99 per cent of our business is outside Ireland and we are focused on a relatively narrow market sector. However, within the food service industry we are well known and we would be seen as probably one of the biggest kitchen equipment suppliers who operate on a global basis. While McDonald's is our biggest customer, there is no formal contract – it's a relationship based on performance. 'We're only as good as our last restaurant,' is a long-standing H&K mantra. We just keep raising the level of service while giving better value to the customer and this approach pays off – we keep winning awards for being the most outstanding supplier.

There is no reason to assume the business won't just keep growing and developing, if we keep building up new customers and keep innovating. Doing different things for existing customers provides opportunities for growth. So for people like McDonald's, as well as supplying kitchens we now do total project management, making extensive use of web-based technology. On the recent launch of a new product in the United States we managed all the construction as well as the kitchen installation.

The underlying philosophy is just to keep doing things well and keep looking for new ways to serve the customer – driving down costs and being extremely competitive. We have a very strong culture in the business – a very non-political perform-ance-based culture. People who don't perform aren't tolerated. At any level, starting with the management, there's no room for non-performance. It's a very driven kind of culture. Recruiting the right people and keeping them is critical to maintaining this culture. The key members of our manage-ment team are mostly in their mid-forties and have been with us for twenty years. While kitchen equipment doesn't sound very glamorous, H&K is an exciting company to work for with great opportunities for bright energetic people.

We are now working on a transnational basis – if we are de-livering a package of equipment into a restaurant in Australia, that equipment might be designed in Dallas and manufactured in Mexico. The purchasing and financial management, on the other hand, would be done out of Dublin, while some of the logistics could be handled out of Rugby. It all arrives in the restaurant in Australia on the appointed day without any problem. That's greatly helped by having a common IT plat-form. What we do is focus particular activities where they can be done best and most cost-effectively. Our lowest cost manu-facturing base is in Mexico. Our management and logistic strengths are in Europe and our main engineering resource is in Dallas. Rather than duplicating all of these, it's a matter of using systems to leverage individual strengths into the whole and coordinating the final product to its final delivery destination. In the last couple of years David Bobbett has been further developing his management approach and restructuring the responsibilities of his team to a flatter model with less emphasis on regional and group hierarchies.

It's the same with people. You find their strengths, rather than focusing too much on their qualifications. It doesn't make that much of a difference whether people start as accountants or lawyers or metal bashers. What matters is that, as they move through their career, they demonstrate they have a good head for managing operations and responding to challenges. Training is important, but you need to pick the right people, the people who have the energy and capability in them, the people who have the attitude and the will for the task, and after that you inculcate in them an understanding of how to manage the business issues.

An aspect of management which features at H&K is giving executives autonomy – push them off the edge, so they're forced to fly. Brief them, mandate them, trust them and, thereafter, let them at it. It's amazing what people can achieve. One thing we have always avoided is any kind of a blame culture. The only criticism you'll get in our operation is for not doing something. If somebody takes an initiative, tackles it and it doesn't quite work out, the attitude is 'OK, put it behind us, let's go.' Openness, honesty and being positive about failure are strong elements in our corporate culture.

With the extensive travel and very demanding customers, our managers put in long hours. However, the rewards are good and, when they perform, the salaries and bonuses are generous and for some there is a prospect of acquiring a stake in the company. It's more than a job. If you're very good at what you do, you acquire an ownership in the company and when you eventually exit, you can walk away with something. It's not unlike a legal or accounting partnership in the way it operates. We find that greatly reinforces the commitment of managers to the business, because it's their business. You think differently when you have a stake in an operation.

Outsiders looking at the H&K business often comment negatively on the fact that it's such a niche business with a single customer (McDonald's) delivering 85 per cent of our revenues, all based on a handshake agreement. The reality is that having one big customer, if the customer is as dispersed and constantly growing as McDonald's, is the same as if we had dozens of customers. We are not dealing with one single Mr McDonald's. We are dealing with McDonald's UK. We are dealing with McDonald's France. We are dealing with McDonald's Australia, McDonald's Singapore and sixty other countries. Each and every one of them is an individual business with its own personality, its own attitudes, and its own needs.

As well as dealing with individual markets, the relationship has to be managed on a global basis. That requires regular contact with senior management in Chicago when we have the opportunity to present our global strategy and align our plans with the customer's needs. Outstanding service is not enough – there must be a global vision for our business as a long-term supplier in order to ensure that we are perceived as a dynamic, progressive company. Backing that up, we must perform better than anybody else in each market so that individual market relationships stand. Depending so much on one customer requires us to be more competitive and standards-driven, constantly anticipating their next need. Part of our success is that we are never complacent about it. We just know that we've got to do the job for them and do it really well – all of the time.

We've made mistakes at various points in our history. Years ago, for example, we were kicked out of the French market for not doing a good job. We learned a great deal from that experience. We put things right and for several years now we have been the dominant player in that market. In 2002, almost immediately after we had taken on a big loan to buy out Gerry, we experienced a sudden downturn in sales which was very embarrassing, as the projections we had presented for the bank had to be trimmed back by as much as 50 per cent. However, with everyone working together to reorganise the business and reduce costs, we got back on track remarkably quickly. Being an approved supplier with a good track record for delivering quality and service is just the beginning. The level of competition to stay on top with a major customer is enormous. H&K has to constantly strive to be ahead, not just of potential competition, but of the thinking within the client company.

In the mid 1990s, we thought it was time to go into China. Every other company seemed to be setting up there. We set up an operation in partnership with a Hong Kong Chinese company and took 50 per cent interest in two plants – one in Shanghai, one in Guangzhou. We worked very hard at it and I was backwards and forwards constantly, visiting China many times in any one year. China has come a long way in the last twelve years and we probably went in too early. What we didn't fully grasp, at that stage, was the difference in how our Chinese partners viewed the deal – 'I win, you lose,' was their idea of partnership.

While our Chinese partners were great to deal with on a personal basis, they just wanted to get our technology and access to our global customer relationships. The two plants were very basic and still very much rooted in the old thinking of the communist system. After eighteen months we came to the conclusion that there was no way we could ever make money. Rather than ploughing in more investment and more management time to try and make it work, we just cut our losses and walked away. We wrote off less than a million dollars in the whole exercise, which means we got off fairly lightly, and we also learned a lot about doing business in the Asia Pacific region. A few years later we went into a licensed manufacturing arrangement in Indonesia, which has been successful, and we are currently edging our way back into the Chinese market. What we have done in Indonesia, and in China the second time around, is on a very different business model to our first Chinese adventure. Control of design, quality and delivery as well as control of the customer relationships are our key requirements, and we avoid the 'handcuffs' of an investment in local buildings and machinery.

For the last few years I have been easing out of the business, and when David Bobbett took over as CEO my focus became more on shareholder issues than on the day-to-day running of the business. It's a great luxury to be in that position – sixty and semi-retired – and it has come about because there are so many good people in our company taking care of the day-to-day details, and they do a tremendous job driving the business forward. In addition, I simply got tired of travelling. Leading a global customer relationship for over twenty years was long enough. We have young people now in the business who see travelling to the far side of the world and coming back as just part of the routine, part of the job, so they're the people who now do that. For them it is all about operational excellence driven by a team of professionals, subscribing to the unique H&K culture with an emphasis on communication, honesty and an expectation of high standards.

Our sales are now close to $400 million. H&K is in good health, with stable ownership, an experienced and ambitious management team, and a 20 per cent per annum growth objective supported by adequate financing. We have come a long way since those turbulent days in the 1980s, and it has all been due to a great a team effort, involving a lot of talented energetic, highly-skilled people. The future looks great for H&K, with our strong global positioning and constant focus on innovation and competitiveness. Although I am now just standing on the touchline, cheering on the team, it is great to have an ongoing involvement with such a great bunch of players.

GALWAY COUNTY LIBRARIES

It's in the Bag

James and Chloe O'Connor, Stronghold

A t this stage, it's everywhere. Not just in Ireland, but in many countries worldwide. Our GreenBag. Our response to government indications, back in 2001, that the ubiquitous plastic shopping bag faced a limited future. Someone opens the hatchback on their car and we see our bags in a neat little pile, folded flat. Someone pushes a supermarket trolley, and there they are: four or five of them, ready to take the week's shopping.

Ireland got used to the GreenBag so fast, it's difficult for most people to remember a time when they didn't exist. We suspect people who use them think that they've been around forever. But they haven't. They were created by us. A well-established family business in Sandyford, Dublin. Our GreenBag was the very first of its type to market in the world. It caught on like wildfire, not just because of the plastic bag levy brought in on 4 March 2002, but because it *worked*. It made sense to customers. It was so much more than a substitute for the old plastic bags. Along with the environmental benefits, it was easier to use, easier to stack in the boot of a car without everything tipping in every direction. And, for the supermarket owners, it was another source of income.

My father Tony worked for a company named Hely's in Dublin, which was bought out by Smurfits in the early 1960s. He continued to work with them until the early 70s, by which time he was about sixty. At an age when most people are considering retiring, he decided it was time to set up his own business, T.S. O'Connor, starting off with his £900 severance sum. He bought a van and traveled the highways and byways of Ireland, selling self-adhesive tape, paper wrapping, twine and plastic bags – anything related to packaging.

In the early 1970s I was doing a B. Comm in UCD. I used to look after the books for him and I could see that it was going quite well, but was probably getting a bit more than he was able for. I approached him about joining the business.

'I'll give you a six months' trial,' he told me. 'Selling. As a rep.'

Now, *there's* an appealing prospect for a young man who's just finished his degree, got married and is working in the Eastern Health Board in a drug addiction unit.

But I could see his point. There was only him and my mother for him to support so he didn't want any extra overheads if it wasn't going to benefit him. Despite the fact that it wasn't much of an offer, I took it. In the first six months I doubled the business. Knocking on doors. Talking to people. I loved it. I loved it because I knew I was good at it because the orders started coming in.

Polythene was just emerging onto the market as a packaging medium for shopping bags. It was used for packing goods in factories; overwrapping goods, shrinkwrapping cans. And, of course, I'd seen that film, *The Graduate*, where the character played by Dustin Hoffman gets career advice from a businessman named McGuire.

'I want to say one word to you,' McGuire tells the young graduate. 'Just one word. Plastics.'

I wouldn't say I was influenced by a film, but I definitely believed there was a great future in plastics, although it still took me a number of years before I understood, every February or March, that the world was not going to end just because the orders weren't flying in at the start of the year. Those first couple of months were always grim. But we had less overheads than the big guys so, although the business was small, it improved steadily, doubling again and again.

After my father died in 1984, I saw an opportunity to buy a unit in Sandyford industrial estate so we moved there and, funnily enough, things seemed to get better with the change of address.

'Oh, we're now based in Sandyford,' I'd tell clients, and for some reason the location seemed to have a positive effect and the business continued to grow. We are still a small core group of people working in the company – eight people – as all of our production is done by third parties and we want to try and keep it around this level.

Around 2000, there was talk of introducing a levy on plastic bags, because they were so polluting, but not much information from the government about how it was going to be implemented. Then we got a phone call from a designer working for Superquinn. Now, any call from Superquinn about bags was interesting, but this one was particularly interesting because as a senator, Fergal Quinn saw that there was a strong possibility that a consumer tax on plastic bags would be introduced. The designer met me one sunny summer evening with a couple of drawings.

'I've been retained by Superquinn to have a look at producing a reusable bag for shopping in Ireland,' he told me. 'Are you interested?'

'That sounds good,' I said. 'Show me what you're thinking of, design-wise.'

So he laid out his rough drawings of supermarket trolleys and how they envisaged putting four or five bags on the base of a trolley and perhaps sitting another four or five on top of those. But, in addition to fitting in the trolley, they wanted bags that could be brought to the back of the checkout and hung while sitting on a base and filled by the shop packers.

'Here's the design brief,' the designer told me. 'Produce something reusable, that fits in nicely with the logistics of a trolley and checkout operation. Quickly.'

I immediately contacted a woman I knew who ran an American company that had connections with manufacturers of PVC suit covers and blanket storage cubes.

'You know what you need,' she said, 'you need canvas or some fabric like that.'

She sent me something but I didn't think it was what we needed. However, it started me thinking. I was familiar with non-woven polypropylene (PP) as a fabric. It was a soft fabric used in the medical business and in the furniture business. What I liked about non-woven polypropylene was that it was soft to the touch. It was used as a liner for such things as babies' nappies, medical gowns and facial wipes. However, I had also seen it used in the furniture industry as a fabric for backing furniture and covering ticking in mattresses. I knew that there were grades of this non-woven PP strong enough to produce as a fabric for shopping bags.

I had a meeting with a friend from Taiwan, whom I'd met by chance in Birmingham at an exhibition.

'Do you know any manufacturers in China who can make this fabric?' I asked him. He nodded.

'Do you know manufacturers who can get samples to us?' He nodded.

'Quickly?' I asked. He nodded.

Superquinn had decided they wanted to put the new bag into just one of their supermarkets for a trial run, in order to get customer feedback. They chose Ballinteer as representative of their customer base, and within weeks they were giving a defined group of customers between 600 and 800 of the bags we had produced. Each customer got five to ten bags; they were asked to do their weekly shopping with them and give feedback.

Out of that research, we built up a body of knowledge about their exact requirement. The material was tweaked. The size was tweaked. The shape of the handles was tweaked. The really important thing was being able to carry these bags when they were full of groceries because not everybody drove to the supermarket. Those customers wanted to be able to fit all their weekly shopping into four or five of these bags instead of having twenty of them.

'But at the same time,' the customers told us, 'we need to be able to carry each individual bag very easily.'

Seven to ten kilos is probably what most customers would be comfortable lifting with one hand. So that determined the capacity and strength.

'If I'm going to carry a fairly heavy weight of groceries in this bag,' another customer said, 'I need you to keep the base of the bag rigid so I can pack it in a block.'

That made sense. It also made sense that if the thing stayed in an oblong shape; it would be easier to pack in the boot of a car together with several others, if a customer was doing a 'big shop'. So we designed a flexible insert made from recycled polyethylene. This was seen as a great benefit because you could put things like juice cartons, cereal packets and similar items into the base and make best use of the space. The design feature of four little silver grommets was the brainchild of Superquinn's designer because they were going to use these at the back of checkouts to hang on. They then became an iconic thing. I'm not sure that they were ever used.

One of Superquinn's requirements was that using these bags should not delay operations at the checkout. Very quickly, Fergal Quinn was getting feedback that the bag actually *enhanced* the operation because this non-woven polypropylene material was semi-rigid. Even though it was very soft and collapsible, it would also stand up as an open bag. It meant you could fill it with two hands instead of always having to take out a bag from under the counter, fiddle it open and pack it with your goods.

That also gave it an advantage over any of the traditional

re-usables, like straw and net bags. Even cotton bags didn't have enough rigidity to stand up to the test at the checkout, and that was a very important feature for them.

Superquinn at that stage were probably using in the region of forty million plastic bags each year, which was a considerable cost. Once he understood that the tax was to be a consumer tax, Fergal Quinn obviously made the decision that this was not only an opportunity to have an alternative to the bag but was also going to be a profit centre and he placed an order. Once the work was done on getting the spec exactly as he wanted, Superquinn placed an order for one million pieces, which they wanted to have *in situ* when the tax became law in March of 2002. We met that deadline.

Those first bags were branded 'Superquinn' and carried a little leaf they'd had designed which became a trademark for them. Later, they moved from the green bag image to a black bag, which we supply in considerable quantities. It has now become a regular shelf item like any other consumer product they sell.

For us, it was a major breakthrough. We were first in the world with a product that worked, at a time when that product was becoming more and more necessary.

T.S. O'Connor took a stand at the global retail trade fair, Euroshop, in Dusseldorf in 2005. Held every three years, the fair brings together more than 1,600 exhibitors from some fifty countries, in what has become known as the premier innovations platform and trend barometer for the retail industry. It proved to be a hugely successful in the development of the GreenBag. At the show, the company made

contact with retailers from over forty-three countries interested in the GreenBag.

At around the same time a leading North American dis-
tributor made contact with T.S. O'Connor about our 'Green-
Bag' programme. The company was planning to launch a
'Bring Your Own Bag' (BYOB) campaign in Canada and the
US in early 2006 and were impressed with T.S. O'Connor,
our innovative products, dedication to quality and strong associations with leading suppliers in China and the Far East. At
this point, we decided to set up a new company, Stronghold
Packaging Distributors Ltd (Stronghold) to manage developing trends and sales of reusable bags worldwide. The Canadian
company appointed Stronghold as the official supplier for the
BYOB programme, sourcing quality products and researching
innovative new reusable packaging concepts.

Stronghold now supply GreenBags to many of North
America's biggest supermarket chains such as Krogers,
Wegmans, A&P, Overwaitea, Shoppers Drug Mart, Topco
and Top Value. Some of the names wouldn't be familiar in
Ireland. Take the Brookshire Brothers Group. Nobody here
has ever heard of them. But they have more than 150 supermarkets in Texas. Which makes for sizeable orders.

In addition, our little bag helped one Canadian town, Leaf
Rapids, become the first town in North America to ban all
plastic bags. The company now exports over twelve million
reusable bags annually to North America, the EU and the
UK. And, all the while, our T.S. O'Connor parent company
continues to serve the domestic market with non-woven shopping bags, paper carrier bags and other packaging supplies.

Superquinn put no overt restrictions on us, but I felt it was decent to let them have a lead time of a year before we sold the product elsewhere in the Irish market. The big disadvantage we had was that you really can't copyright or patent a shopping bag, so when we went to China to one of the fairs about two years later, we saw maybe twenty or thirty groups of manufacturers or agents selling this exact bag. They weren't calling it a green bag, but it was this exact size and shape of bag.

On the other hand, in 2005 in Germany at Euroshop, an exhibition dealing with everything to do with supermarkets other than food, we were the only exhibitors showing a genuinely reusable bag. We met people from the biggest supermarkets in the world who were interested.

All of this was changing the scale, scope and reach of our company, and I needed to strengthen its management. At this stage, Chloe, my daughter, was working in the IT & Telephones department at UCD.

'Look, there is an opportunity here,' I told her. 'What I would like you to do is come and learn about the business if you want to. You can start doing secretarial duties, answering the phone, getting to know the customers, getting to know the products. That's the best way to do it. There's not going to be any formal training. It's going to be hands on.'

I knew she was very bright and I knew from her social and personal skills that she would actually be very good at selling as well. I also thought that she was good at managing things. I'm glad to say that I was vindicated in my decision. Not only has she proven to be very good at managing, she's also good on deadlines and details in a way I'm not, so we complement each other. Above all, though, she loves meeting people face to face, talking about the products we sell, trying to make them interested. She loves the buzz of trade shows and does them on her own, even in China.

Chloe brought enthusiasm and business experience with her – together with a sensibility around human rights, having done voluntary work for Amnesty International. We visit every factory that we deal with in China and we have a group called FWC (Fair Working Conditions) which audits factories on request. They visit and certify many of the factories that we deal with. The image of China as being a sweatshop is probably a little bit outdated. I'm sure there are practices in some areas – like toy and clothing industries – where bad practices happen, but in most of the areas we deal with, the workforce is now very well educated. Thirty-three million Chinese do the equivalent of the Leaving Cert every year, and all of them want to go on to third level. Four to five hundred million people there constitute a burgeoning middle class. At one small fair, we met a manufacturer of grand pianos making 1,100 grand pianos a week, not for the export market. These were for sale only in China. Things are changing in China, but we always ensure who we deal with comes up to our standards of fair trading.

The GreenBag, and the call from Superquinn were incredibly fortuitous in our development. To put it in context, a number of people I knew and had done business with for many years actually went out of business or were seriously damaged by the introduction of the plastic bag levy, mainly because they just weren't focused on the fact that this was going to happen. Or, in some cases, they thought it was an opportunity to make money by bringing in container loads of plastic bags because they thought they could beat the tax by selling them in advance. It wasn't really clear from the government that this was something the *consumer* would have to pay for. In addition, a lot of goods previously on order were still coming into the country. We had one major customer who had ordered a hundred thousand polythene bags. They were a retail outlet as opposed to a supermarket and I advised them not to bring maybe £10,000 worth of goods in. But they brought the goods in January and they were using them. Then on the 2nd March nobody would take a bag from them because they had to charge 15c for it.

In theory, Britain should have been a great market for the GreenBag, particularly because I was quite familiar with the English market and had talked to a few people in the UK about the possibility of reusable bags. They didn't think anything would happen there because of the presence of the British Plastics Association Federation, which had huge vested interests both in manufacturing in the UK and in the Far East. No major British group apart from Sainsbury's and Morrison's have done anything significant in the reusable bag business. Although, that may change now that Gordon Brown has said that it's on his agenda. But, for instance, in Scotland the First Minister shot it down. They took a decision that they wouldn't ban or impose a tax on plastic bags, mainly because of the heavy lobbying by the British polythene industries.

The failure of the UK market to come on board had nothing to do with us being an indigenous Irish business.

Generally, that has been a great advantage, despite our small size. In remote areas of China I have encountered people who run factories who ask me where I'm from.

'Oh, Ireland,' they say, eyes lighting up. 'Oh, you have such economic growth.'

They can tell you the GDP and the growth rate for the last ten years. Even though their own success is phenomenal, they are very conscious that in Europe we seem to be the leading lights. But, quite apart from China, worldwide, being Irish is a good thing. We're liked. We're seen as great craic, while at the same time being honest. Which is the way Chloe and I see our own business. It sounds a bit corny, but we stress mutual respect and I can truthfully say that we are honest in all our dealings with both our suppliers and our customers. If people make mistakes that are to our advantage we have no problem telling them that and we expect the same thing to be offered to us.

We've already moved on, in terms of innovation. We developed a Coolbag, made from a similar material to the GreenBag but lined with aluminium and EPE (expanded polyethylene), which serves as either a picnic bag or a bag for keeping cold goods bought in a supermarket. We also developed a bag that would hold six bottles of wine, made from the same material.

In addition, a couple of years ago we were approached by a Canadian company to have a look at developing a bag that had a 20 to 30 per cent recycled post consumer content. They were particularly interested in recycled bottles, PET bottles: the big Coca-Cola, soft drink and water bottles. Those bottles are a major issue, because they occupy the same bulk empty as they do full. Hence, they are a huge disposal problem.

We began to research this, quickly discovering one company that had a fabric made from recycled post consumer PET fibres. (PET is the name for the material that's used in plastic bottles. It's polyester but is referred to as PET.) I went to places where PET bottles were crushed and baled, then chipped and washed, and finally melted and extruded into tiny little fibres. These fibres were already being used to produce fleece jackets.

'If they're doing that,' I thought, 'there must be a way of making a fabric for reusable bags.'

There was. We have devised this product and we're now producing a bag that's black when made from coloured bottles and white when clear bottles are used. We're very excited by this because it is truly recycled *and* recyclable. We have also achieved an 85 per cent post consumer recycled content. I've branded it with a play on words: 'The bottles are in the bag', because I thought that somebody like Coca-Cola or Pepsi would like such an idea for carrying newly purchased soft drinks. We think it's a great marketing story because in every one of these new bags are twelve 500ml post consumer recycled bottles.

The two of us like to see ourselves at the developing edge of reusable packaging products for shopping. That's the area of the business I tend to concentrate on, now that Chloe has taken over much of the managing. Plus, of course, I deal with approaches from companies who are interested in buying us out. I don't want to sell the business, though. Because I enjoy what I'm doing and Chloe enjoys it just as much. I have purposely kept the business at a size we're comfortable with, having seen what big business can do to people.

There's a delicate balance to be drawn between wanting to be hugely successful and wanting your own time as well.

GALWAY COUNTY LIBRARIES